THE ROYAL COMMISSION ON HISTORICAL MANUSCRIPTS

ARCHIVE BUILDINGS IN THE UNITED KINGDOM 1977–1992

THE ROYAL COMMISSION ON HISTORICAL MANUSCRIPTS

Archive Buildings in the United Kingdom 1977–1992

Christopher Kitching

LONDON: HMSO

Cover
The cover illustration is based on a design elevation of
the Nottinghamshire Archives building, reproduced
by kind permission of the architects, Corstorphine and
Wright.

Contents

Illustrations   vi

Preface   vii

Introduction   1

Part 1

1.   Archives and archive buildings: the nature of the challenge   5

2.   The site   13

3.   Structure and materials: general considerations   17

4.   Structure and materials: particular features   25

5.   Security against vandalism and theft   33

6.   Fire prevention   39

7.   Environmental control   45

8.   Conversion of existing buildings   53

9.   Functions: some practical hints   61

Bibliography   75

Part 2: Case Studies   79

Appendix: list of archive buildings 1977–1992   141

Synopsis of subjects in Part 1   143

Illustrations

Unless otherwise indicated, the illustrations have been supplied by, and are reproduced by kind permission of, the respective record repositories.

Part 1

1. Northamptonshire Record Office under construction. 8
2. West Sussex Record Office. 14
3. Medieval head from excavations at Lambeth Palace Library. *Andy Chopping, Museum of London.* 15
4. Cheshire Record Office, showing the building's steel frame. 18
5. Installing a suspended ceiling, Doncaster Archives Department. 26
6. The roof void at Suffolk Record Office, Ipswich. 27
7. Blocked-up windows, Doncaster Archives Department. 29
8. Steel roller-doors protecting the entrance to the Post Office Archives. 31
9. Halon gas cylinders, Walsall Archives Service. 41
10. The exhibition room at the Public Record Office, Chancery Lane. *Museum design, John Dangerfield Associates; specialist fibre optics Absolute Actions of London; photograph by Marianne Majerus.* 52
11. Converted warehouse: Bristol Record Office. 56
12. Converted warehouse: Cheshire Record Office. 56
13. Converted church: Hampshire Record Office (to 1993). 59
14. The reception area at Lincolnshire Archives. 63
15. Map storage: Cornwall Record Office. 64
16. Map storage: West Sussex Record Office. 65
17. Mobile racking at Suffolk Record Office, Ipswich. *Stelstor.* 65
18. Conservation workshop at Lincolnshire Archives. 67

Part 2

The illustrations in Part 2, which refer to the respective case studies, are uncaptioned. Grateful acknowledgement is made to the respective governing authorities and archivists in charge. Additional acknowledgements: Lancashire (*Norwyn Photographics*), Museum of Science and Industry in Manchester (*Della Batchelor*), Public Record Office (*Crown copyright*).

Preface

The Commission has a nationwide responsibility under its Royal Warrant of 1959 'to promote and assist the proper preservation and storage of manuscripts and records'. For this reason as well as through its statutory responsibility to inspect repositories which the Master of the Rolls may wish to recognise for the custody of Manorial and Tithe Documents it has been privileged to advise many custodians in both public and private sectors on matters connected with archival accommodation. The challenges have ranged from advice *in situ* about individual problems to the critical scrutiny of plans for wholly new repositories or the quest for suitable buildings for adaptation.

This study of archive buildings throughout the country over the past decade and a half has a three-fold purpose:

- to record the considerable progress made by custodians and their governing authorities in improving standards in line with the British Standard recommendations for the *Storage and exhibition of archival documents* (BS 5454), first published in 1977 and revised in 1989;

- to share with a wider readership the commoner problems and pitfalls observed by, or reported to, the Commission during the period, and at the same time see what lessons may be learnt from them; and

- to offer short illustrated case studies of some of the buildings, and thereby to atone for the remarkable paucity of British documentation in this field.

The overall objective is to promote still better standards and encourage those who are striving to attain them. For its part, the Commission will continue to support their endeavours, to share its long experience, and to offer advice where this may be helpful.

Grateful acknowledgement is made for the assistance so readily given by many custodians in the course of this study, and their generosity not only in answering many questions but also in supplying the illustrations. I am particularly indebted to Brian Smith, Richard Olney, David Vaisey, Andrew Broom, Patrick Cadell, Jean Elrington, and David Thomas who kindly commented on the text in draft.

CJ Kitching
Secretary

Quality House, Quality Court,
Chancery Lane, London WC2A 1HP

Introduction

The year 1977 chosen as the departure point for this study of public archive buildings saw the publication, after years of deliberation by experts, of the first edition of British Standard 5454, *Recommendations for the storage and exhibition of archival documents* and the opening of the new Public Record Office at Kew. That building, whose designers had used drafts of the Standard, may be regarded as the first repository of a new era in which BS 5454 has called the tune. It remains by far the largest purpose-built archive repository in the United Kingdom, and has been the pace-setter of its generation.

Fifteen years on, it is time to take an objective look at the influence of the British Standard, now into its second edition (1989). In the intervening period we have witnessed a remarkable transformation in the stock of public-sector archive buildings. Progress, it is true, has not been spread evenly throughout the country, and problems have been encountered on the way even in the flagship repositories. This volume seeks both to celebrate what has been achieved and to air some of those problems, openly but not accusingly.

★

A number of other factors need to be taken into account alongside the British Standard in explaining the growing concern to provide our archives with the best possible protection. Some of these have roots in an earlier period. Public and institutional awareness of the importance and utility of archives – in common with every other aspect of our heritage – has been growing, especially since the Second World War, and with it the demand both for archive storage accommodation and for facilities for public access. As a direct consequence a network of public and private archive reposi-

tories came to be established throughout the country, mainly between the 1940s and 1970s; the Society of Archivists was founded in 1947, and the first postgraduate diploma courses in archives administration were offered at University College London and at Liverpool University in the same year. Nor is the profession in Britain isolated from developments in other countries. There is greater international exchange of professional ideas today than ever before, through the International Council on Archives, through bi-lateral contacts, and through the sharing of technical information and experience in the professional literature and at national and international conferences.

So there is a substantial and rapidly growing body of evidence on the conditions in which archives flourish or deteriorate, and on the measures which may be said to promote or compromise their wellbeing. Together, we have identified most of their known enemies, which are unfortunately becoming more, not less, numerous if we consider such recent worldwide additions as atmospheric pollution, nuclear radiation, terrorism and civil disorder, and nearer home a small but not negligible incidence of vandalism.

This in turn means that we are rightly more demanding in the standards we set and accept. The necessarily *ad hoc* arrangements for many of the first generation of post-war record repositories – very largely established in town and county administrative offices – were the best that could be achieved in the circumstances of the time, the place and the economy. They served in some cases for thirty years or more. But, as illustrated in Chapter 1, the records themselves have set the agenda for change by their inexorable tendency to fill up their accommodation. In rapid succession in the period under review one repository after another had to extend its storage or make entirely new provision. With rare exceptions this was undertaken in full awareness that the ground-rules had changed since the services were first set up; and that arrangements which took no account of BS 5454 could not stand up to critical scrutiny when the quality and cost-effectiveness of all services were under review.

★

BS 5454 put the United Kingdom well to the fore worldwide in standards for archive accommodation. Its recommendations have been promoted as best practice since 1977 by the three bodies which for certain statutory purposes inspect and approve record repositories: the Public Record Office (on behalf of the Lord Chancellor in respect of locally held Public Records), the Scottish Record Office (in respect of records under the charge and super-intendence of the Keeper of the Records of Scotland), and the Royal Commission on Historical Manuscripts (on behalf of the Master of the Rolls in respect of Manorial and Tithe Documents). The Standard was revised in the 1980s and a new edition published in 1989.[1] It forms the basis of the Guidelines for Record Repositories issued by the three inspecting bodies.[2]

The Standard has been widely brought to the attention of architects and engineers planning new archive accommodation, and there can be no doubt at all that it has been influential and beneficial. It should perhaps be noted that like other British Standards BS 5454 is advisory not mandatory. It does not have the force of law. Nor can its every clause taken in isolation be quoted as the last word on its subject. There was considerable discussion on a number of aspects of BS 5454 in the course of its revision in the 1980s, for example over:

- whether windows were desirable in the repository;

- whether it was essential to provide automatic means of fire-extinction;

- whether water-sprinklers were an acceptable means of fire-fighting in a repository;

- whether wood was an acceptable material for shelving and doors.

On all these points there remains some debate among the experts. The issues cannot be judged in isolation from the circumstances of the individual repository and the whole package of measures proposed for its protection. Healthy questioning of this kind is likely to continue as more scientific knowledge and long-term experience become available to draw on. But BS 5454 may be said to represent the best attainable consensus among British experts.

★

Among other trends or concerns of the period, which no current designer of archive accommodation can ignore, the following may be singled out.

(i) *Energy-consciousness*. The steep increases in oil prices in the 1970s and growing concern in recent years over the effects on the global environment of burning fossil fuels stimulated research into building design and insulation, with a view to reducing dependence on power.

(ii) *Security*. A spate of notorious thefts of records in the 1980s, and isolated incidents since, leave no room for complacency over security, whether in the design of archive buildings or in the provision of appropriate invigilation and security equipment. Vandalism too is unfortunately on the increase.

(iii) *Health and safety*. The period has seen far-reaching concern for health and safety, the provision of facilities for the disabled, and the control of substances hazardous to health. Most noticeably, fumigation of records in the battle against mould has been largely discontinued on health and safety grounds but also because its efficacy has been questioned. Rooms once set aside for this purpose have been turned into drying or isolation rooms. There have been health alerts over such newly-identified hazards as legionnaires' disease, 'humidifier fever' and 'sick building syndrome', all of which have implications for the design and maintenance of environmental controls for the good of people as well as records.

(iv) *Consumer trends*. Although at the time of writing the number of reader-visits to some repositories seems to have reached a plateau after the sharp increases of the 1970s and 1980s, numbers generally continue to rise. With growing demand for access to original historical source materials to support teaching at all levels from primary schools to universities and for the group visits and lectures which go with such programmes; and also with predictions that the amount of leisure time will continue to increase, the provision of adequate space for the public in record offices remains a priority.

(v) *New media*. The much-heralded 'paperless office' is not yet upon us. Vast quantities of paper-based archives will continue to accrue for the foreseeable future. But alongside these there are already signs of a growing need to care for records in other media: photographs, movie film, magnetic tape and electronic media. These cannot all simply be stored alongside the traditional paper and parchment. They require different environmental controls. It remains a matter for each governing body whether to provide these special facilities and the equipment necessary to 'read' or play back the archives in question. The expense involved – the more so as archives in these media accrue – may be a powerful argument in favour of contracting out such services to specialist organisations or sharing facilities in a deliberately restricted number of repositories equipped for the job. But where they are to be kept, the custodian has to pay attention to the specific conditions required by each medium, and the appropriate means for their consultation.

(vi) *Preservation*. The rapid increase in security microfilming and the production to the public of copies rather than originals of the most frequently used records, is altering the space requirements for machinery and equipment in reading rooms.

★

In 1983 the Association of County Archivists noted that 'many repositories in this country accept documents into supposedly safe custody for storage in conditions which fall far short of the established British Standard'.[3] The Society of Archivists reached the same conclusion with regard to storage areas:

> Few are purpose-built; many are inadequately provided with fire precautions, humidity and temperature controls or air filtration . . . . Neither owners of records nor the public can feel secure that our archival heritage is being cared for adequately.[4]

In 1985 the Commission carried out a survey of publicly-funded record repositories [Smith]. A fifth of all respondents felt that their principal storage accommodation fell below standard whilst over four-fifths expected their storage to be full within five years. Severe constraints upon public expenditure during the 1970s and 1980s appeared to have taken a heavy toll.

And yet the picture was not uniformly gloomy. Some governing authorities had succeeded, even in the generally leaner years, in making capital provision to improve their archive accommodation. Although no nationwide trend was discernible at the time, the pace of improvement was already accelerating in the early 1980s as more and more of the first generation of record offices reached full capacity, as the pattern of archive service provision following restructuring of local government in the 1970s took firmer shape, and as new points of outreach were established in branch record offices and libraries.

Taking the whole period 1977–1992, over one hundred publicly-funded record repositories are known to the Commission to have been built, extended or substantially refurbished. A representative selection of these is described in Part 2 and a check-list is provided in the Appendix. Still others are on the drawing board. On the other hand some governing bodies still await the resources, or the vision, to promote the kind of improvements that would bring their accommodation up to standard; and indeed the standard of those which have simply stood still in this period has fallen in comparison with the continuously rising 'national average'. Nevertheless the conclusion is inescapable: we have much to be proud of, and to celebrate. The challenge now is to build on this foundation and ensure that, as the present trustees of the records, we hand them down to future generations in excellent shape.

★

This is the first book about archive buildings in Britain. It takes the story on from where Lionel Bell's formative article on 'Archival accommodation in the United Kingdom' [Bell, 1980] left off. With the exception of the Public Record Office few modern British archive buildings have attracted significant attention in the professional literature or the press. This is in direct contrast with libraries, whose development has been impressively charted in the periodic volumes on *Public library buildings* [Harrison 1987, 1990] and in many monographs, among which might be singled out Alan Konya's *Libraries: a briefing and design guide* (1986).

It would be unthinkable to embark on any serious study in this field without paying homage to Michel Duchein's *Archive buildings and equipment* (1st edn 1966), of which a second revised and enlarged edition, translated into English by David Thomas, was published by the International Council on Archives (ICA) in 1988. Through its journal *Archivum* the ICA has a long record of promoting the study of archive buildings worldwide and collecting and comparing professional experience, culminating in a recent study of *Modern buildings of national archives* [Archivum, 1986]. Among other international publications may be mentioned the proceedings of an expert consultation held in Vienna in 1985 and published in English as 'Archive buildings and the conservation of archival material' by the Austrian national archives in 1986.[5]

In some other European countries archives have had a stronger press. The Direction des Archives de France published in 1986 a detailed study, *Bâtiments d'archives − vingt ans d'architecture française 1965–1985*, whilst several of the individual French purpose-built repositories have promoted their own illustrated books about their buildings and their contents. Similarly in Spain the second volume of Maria del Carmen Pescador del Hoyo's archive manual *El Archivo. Instalación y conservación* (1988) was largely devoted to buildings.

The present volume takes some of its inspiration from all these models. But it owes more to the solid achievements in the United Kingdom since the first publication of BS 5454, and to the efforts of archivists and their governing authorities whose enthusiastic cooperation in this study is most gratefully acknowledged.

1. BS 5454: 1989, *Recommendations for storage and exhibition of archival documents*. Copies are obtainable from the British Standards Institution, Linford Wood, Milton Keynes MK14 6LE.

2. Published as an appendix to *A standard for record repositories* (1990), see bibliography: Royal Commission on Historical Manuscripts.

3. *Yesterday's future* (Association of County Archivists, 1983), pp.5, 9.

4. *Towards a national policy for archives* (Society of Archivists, 1983), p.14.

5. *Mitteilungen des Österreichischen Staatsarchivs*, 39 (1986), pp.197–289.

Chapter 1
Archives and archive buildings: the nature of the challenge

Growing pains

Archives accumulate unrelentingly. There is no turnover of stock as in a lending library or commercial warehouse, but only the continual addition of new items or whole new collections which, like those already held, are intended for permanent preservation. This is true whether by 'archives' we mean simply the historic administrative records of the parent organisation or, as the term is more commonly applied by public repositories, the whole range of material acquired by transfer, gift, purchase, loan or statutory deposit.

Predicting their accrual rate however is notoriously difficult. Annual averages may be useful for forward planning but they can so easily be overtaken by unforeseen events. For example, legislation has repeatedly directed or encouraged the transfer to public repositories of large quantities of records which were previously held elsewhere, as happened in England under the Parochial Registers and Records Measure 1978. The decision by a local authority to introduce a programme for the management of its modern administrative records alongside its archives – as in Staffordshire in 1986/7 or Grampian in 1991[1] has similarly been known to swallow up available storage space. Also, unrepeatable opportunities have arisen quite unexpectedly to acquire large collections of family or business papers by bequest or private treaty sale or at auction.

Some degree of forward planning for growth therefore ought to be a normal commitment on the part of those authorities which offer a public archive service. Regrettably this has often been overlooked or pushed aside by budgetary constraints. Where a new building is required, it will be prudent to allow say five years as the run-in time, to take account of political, financial and planning considerations as well as site acquisition and building. It would be easy to marshal a regiment of archivists' annual reports bearing warnings that the storage space is becoming or has become full with no sign of a solution being devised. What is more, a considerable time can elapse between an authority's being committed to a new building or extension and the day of its eventual occupation. Meanwhile the normal accessioning process is put at risk for want of suitable storage space.

Amid all the competing claims on public funds, archive services have tended to be given low priority. Many of the repositories whose new premises are celebrated in this volume had long been overdue for a move from almost unmanageable circumstances, with records scattered in accommodation inadequate by today's standards, including out-stores remote from the main building and of inferior quality. Others unhappily remain in that plight.

Once an authority accepts that additional or alternative accommodation is required, and commits the necessary capital, it has three main options: to acquire or build one or more out-stores, while retaining the original building; to commission a new, purpose-built repository to hold everything; or to acquire an alternative building for conversion to hold everything.

The choice is not always clear-cut. When the Public Record Office planned its new repository at Kew in the 1970s it decided to retain the existing purpose-built Victorian repository in Chancery Lane as well. Fifteen years later it is to construct a second building at Kew with a view to concentrating its whole operation there. The Scottish Record Office, faced with growing storage problems in its two buildings in central Edinburgh (HM General Register House and West Register House, a converted church), considered (a) abandoning both for a large purpose-built repository; (b) building on an annexe to one of the existing buildings; or (c) retaining both buildings and constructing a third to serve principally for storage. Despite the inconvenience of managing a third building this last option proved to be the most cost-effective. In 1983 Hereford and Worcester had to make the difficult choice between concentrating all its Worcester holdings in a single new purpose-built repository or retaining the use of the former St Helen's church (converted for use by Worcestershire Record Office in 1956) on which it still had 20 years of unexpired lease. It chose to retain the church, which had proved its worth as a repository, and build a new repository in addition.

Good quality out-stores may be a practical and cost-effective solution, especially if reserved mainly for those records which are least in demand. But there has been a marked tendency among the authorities providing archive services to suppose that such auxiliary buildings can with impunity make do with second-rate standards of custody, particularly with regard to security and environmental controls. This is a fallacy. The British Standard recommendations should be seen as applying equally to all the materials which are intended to be preserved permanently.

Where the preferred solution has been not an out-store but a new building, both purpose-building and conversion have had their advocates. Some will find it odd that consideration of the case for and against conversions is deferred here until such a late chapter. But this is quite deliberate. Before looking for solutions we need to know our specifications. To what standards should the building conform? What functions and services must it accommodate both now and in the future? How long is that future to be – 5, 10, 15, 20 years or more? And is there an obvious strategy beyond that? With answers to those kinds of questions to

hand, real planning and the search for a site or building can begin.

In general, to judge by the examples studied, storage capacity has been planned to last for 10 to 25 years depending on the commissioning authority's circumstances and the availability of alternative properties, or of adjacent space, for extension or modular development. Too short a period and the planning and upheaval have to be undertaken again uncomfortably soon; too long and there is a risk of costly accommodation lying idle. On the other hand it is sometimes forgotten that other functions besides storage may expand over a 10 to 20 year period. Allowance has to be made for any foreseeable increases in staff, readership and other public (eg educational) visits, and for changes in technology requiring, for example, additional microfilm readers or computer terminals, and associated cabling.

The best laid plans can be frustrated by events such as the arrival of records in bulk from an unexpected source or by changes to the proposed building scheme on the insistence of the planning authority. The Greater London Record Office (1982) was expected when opened to cater for the authority's archives for 17 years until the lease of an upper floor expired allowing space for expansion. But its governing authority, the Greater London Council, was itself abolished in 1986, and the need to make early provision for its administrative records required a new extension. Bradford (West Yorkshire) saw its hoped-for long-term expansion space on the upper floors of its building sold off. Fire and safety regulations demanded more space than originally anticipated in the plans of Gloucestershire Record Office, with a consequent reduction in archive storage capacity. The original plans for the PRO at Kew were for a building 28 metres high. The planning authority insisted that this be reduced, and the final building rose only 22 metres: a repository intended to last to the end of the century had virtually a decade cut off its useful life.

Time-scale

Even without such upsets, planning can be a lengthy and professionally demanding process. The text-book approach posits time for reflection, research, discussion and refinement, involving all the staff and other prominent stakeholders in the operation and clearing away mutual misconceptions between the funding body, the architect, the archivist and the contractors about the objectives of the exercise, the nature and style of the building, and the financial and other constraints.[2] Typical stages on the way are illustrated in figure 1. In practice, circumstances may demand improvisations, refinements and short-cuts, or additional or repeated stages.

Figure 1
Summary of planning stages.

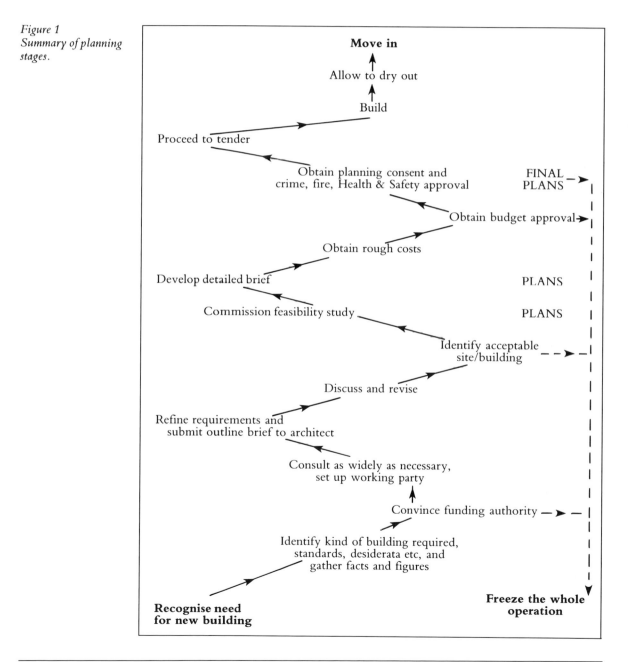

1 *Northamptonshire Record Office under construction.*

For a building of the scale and national importance of the PRO at Kew, planning of course involved a team of experts over a long period, and time to take wide soundings of the needs of readers and of the neighbouring community [Cox p.135]. For smaller repositories the time available for preparing and presenting the case, drafting and revising the plans and seeing the project through has been very variable. A few examples may put this in perspective.

In Dorset the first efforts to identify possible sites for a new record office, between 1982 and 1984, proved abortive, and even though the project became a capital priority in 1986 it was spring 1988 before the right site could be found. Feasibility plans were discussed with the Commission in August that year before being approved by the county's Amenities Committee in the autumn. Budgetary approval was obtained in December. In the winter and spring of 1989 the detailed proposal was approved successively by the county council and the fire officer, and planning permission

obtained. Tenders went out in August 1989, and there was time for an archaeological dig on the site before building began in January 1990. There were few setbacks on the way, largely because the county council was in a position to allow some budgetary flexibility rather than imposing from the outset a tight and unrealistic ceiling on expenditure. The record office opened in April 1991.

Northamptonshire Record Office had already filled Delapre Abbey to capacity by the late 1970s without having devised a longer-term strategy. It took a spell of severe weather in 1986 and a resulting flood to highlight the need for major structural repairs. A threefold choice opened up: to repair and extend the old building, to acquire and convert a building elsewhere, or to build a new record office. The first was ruled out on grounds of cost and difficulties as to ownership. The second was actively explored: a number of buildings were considered for conversion, and in one case feasibility plans were drawn up. The third option did not even seem a starter. Then unexpectedly in September 1988 the sale of some county council property provided the wherewithal to contemplate a new archive building as a timely commemoration of the county council's centenary, provided that the funds could be committed within that financial year. Speed was therefore of the essence. The county archivist worked intensively with the architect for two months to plan a new building from scratch. There could be no extensive consultations, though good use was made of the recent experience of two other counties, West Sussex and Suffolk, in building new repositories. After only three months the job – incorporating at the last minute a new Emergency Control Centre for the county – was ready to go to tender, and an 18-month building programme began in April 1989.

It would be misleading to suggest that planning and execution always proceed so smoothly. In a search for a new branch repository for West Cumbria a brief was first drawn up by the county archivist in November 1981. Suitable premises were found in a former school at Whitehaven. A scheme was designed for its conversion, and planning permission granted in June 1985. But expenditure constraints caused the project to be deferred on the eve of going to tender. Another site, the former police station, became available in 1989, and a successful feasibility study for its conversion was concluded by the same architects. The project again narrowly failed to receive capital funding in 1990 but is now at last under way. Examples like this could be multiplied. Plans which have lain unexecuted for a number of years will almost certainly need review to take account of the most recent developments in design, materials and technology.

Uncertainties over the future development of a service can result in a kind of planning blight, with the funding authority hesitant to commit resources to the refurbishment, or even the maintenance, of the premises until longer-term strategy has been resolved. In the early 1980s, Clwyd county council was for a time considering abandoning the record office in the old rectory at Hawarden and merging all its operations in the branch office at Ruthin. Only after several years of discussion did it decide to retain both. In the meantime, improvements to heating, wiring and car park facilities had to wait. In more than one English city, misty plans for heritage centres which might incorporate the archives along with other services on a new site have been used as an argument against improving existing accommodation. The extension to the PRO at Kew was held up in 1990 pending Treasury approval which in turn had to await the outcome of an efficiency scrutiny, a preliminary to the Office's transition to the status of a government executive agency.

There can be unexpected opportunities too. Walsall archives service's move to its new building was facilitated by the local government reforms of 1985 which caused its former premises to be required for other uses. The record office at Caernarfon was provided with a site for development at short notice, partly in order to hide a multi-storey car park that would otherwise have been an eyesore on the water-front.

Likely cost

It is difficult to judge the final costs until quite late in the planning process, when detailed specifications have been drawn up for building, plant, equipment and furniture, but for budgetary purposes some estimate has to be made. The case studies in part 2 below suggest an average cost in today's terms of between £2- and £3-million for a new purpose-built county record office, excluding the cost of the land. Some authorities have proudly claimed similar results for less than £1-million, mainly on converted buildings. But comparisons are precarious because of differing costing practices and differences in the standards aimed at. It is part of the purpose of this book to highlight those standards and therefore the criteria for measuring whether particular schemes not only offer value for money but also come up to today's expectations for the protection of the nation's written heritage.

Budgetary ceilings have often been imposed that prove unrealistically low in relation to the task in hand, but yet cannot be exceeded. Then, unless contingency or alternative funds may be drawn on or the load spread across several financial years, something has to be foregone, or the whole project abandoned. Discounting any strategic over-bidding for funding and facilities, the governing body has to judge at what level of cutback the central objective of the scheme is compromised. Some have had to settle for a smaller building than originally planned, or for a lesser degree of environmental control or fire protection, to pare down requirements for secondary storage and staff accommodation, or to phase a conversion or the purchase of machinery and equipment over a number of years. The authorities responsible for caring for archives need to be aware of the commitment into which they are entering if they are to make adequate provision to meet their obligations.

What is an archive building like?

Until the present generation, when some recognisable common features such as thick walls and overhanging roofs began to appear in successive new buildings, there was scarcely anything like a distinctive genre of archive buildings in the United Kingdom. Architects in this country, unlike some of those in France, for example, do not specialise in this field because archive buildings are too few in number (compared with, say, libraries or museums) to be encountered more than once in the average career. Nor are architects' reference shelves overflowing with guides to the construction and layout of archive buildings as they might be for libraries. To make matters worse, outside the national repositories archivists have on the whole been diffident about describing their buildings in print, and there is no Central Direction of Archives to insist on standards. Perhaps this lack of a universal solution is a good thing because the differences between the needs of any two authorities commissioning archive buildings may be as significant as the similarities.[3]

But the territory is by no means uncharted. BS 5454 is the first essential point of reference, and there is no shortage of published guidance on planning and briefing specifically for archive buildings, as well as useful comparative material on libraries.[4]

Other sources of guidance that have been influential in the design of several of the buildings described in this volume are the unpublished briefs held by colleagues who have recently gone through a similar exercise, and of course visits to the sites to see how the vision was turned into reality.

★

But all these demonstrate that there is no single 'right' way to build an archive building. The examples selected for study in this book amply testify to the variety of solutions possible in such matters as the overall shape and style of the building and even, to some extent, the use of materials.

There are, however, two fundamental keys to success: and they are more a matter of objectives than of bricks and mortar. Every aspect of an archive building must, in this order, serve (1) to protect the archives against all forces which might otherwise harm them: in particular fire and water, physical or chemical change resulting from a polluted or under-regulated environment; dust, mould and vermin; theft and vandalism; and (2) to promote also the work and wellbeing of everyone (staff and public alike) going about their business there.

An archive building is in a number of important respects *sui generis* precisely because archives themselves are unique and irreplaceable. Therefore it cannot be planned and built as though it were really something else (a library or warehouse, for example). If the chosen course is to convert an existing building, which really *was* something else, the question to be asked at the outset is whether it can match up to its required new character.

★

One question which has a bearing on everything else from the choice of site/ground space required to the shape and layout of the building/number of storeys, its structure and the materials employed, is the preferred approach to the segregation of functions.

Textbooks usually emphasise the desirability of segregating functions that demand different degrees of security, environmental control, fire prevention, human comfort, and so on. The five traditional functional groups are storage, plant, offices, technical services and public areas. As will become apparent from the case studies in part 2, their segregation has been made a virtue in the design and layout of a number of the buildings covered in this survey. And indeed, some degree of segregation is always to be found.

There is no question where the priority must lie: in the provision of secure custody for the records, in a controlled environment. This may seem self-evident, but it is surprising how often it either takes second place to the provision of a public service, or of an aesthetically pleasing building, or to the convenient location of the archive service alongside related services, or else is played down for budgetary reasons. It needs to be reasserted that without the secure custody there may be a risk of theft or damage to some or all of the holdings; without the controlled environment the condition of the records may deteriorate until in extreme cases they become irreparable. In either event there would be a loss or diminution of the resource upon which all the repository's other activities depend.

In positioning functions within the site plan the main concern is to protect the storage area (both laterally and vertically) from all risk of fire, water penetration, unauthorised intrusion, and threats to its internal environment. The first obvious candidates for segregation on these grounds are plant rooms. But documents move around the building, they are not always safely tucked away in the strongroom. And danger may arise elsewhere: from machinery and equipment; from stores of chemicals or flammable materials; from water, drainage and sewerage services, and so on. So segregation is not a universal panacea.

A number of recent new archive buildings, including the county record offices of Dorset, Lancashire, Leicestershire and Suffolk, and indeed some adapted buildings as in Cheshire, have been designed with storage blocks detached from the rest of the building, apart from connecting corridors or bridges. Where such rigorous segregation is impractical, or is rejected on other grounds, attention has been turned to minimising hazards by every other means possible. How this may be done is to be found in subsequent chapters.

Records permanently in store are no 'records' at all: they are there to be consulted. But before this can happen they have to be sorted and described, and thereafter both they and the staff have to be managed. That requires office and work space. Experience unfortunately suggests that this tends to be skimped or to be targeted for savings when budgets have to be trimmed. And yet, where insufficient space is provided for these management functions staff morale can be sharply reduced and the efficiency of the whole operation threatened. Next to the records the staff are the building's most important resource.

The care and management of archives calls in addition for technical facilities such as conservation, reprographics and computer services. These are not always provided in-house, but where they are to be provided they require planning of an order different from the main run of offices, with special attention to health and safety and to the provision of dedicated power, water and other services.

Many would regard public access as the principal purpose for an archive building. The public areas are certainly the most visible, and therefore most likely to attract comment in the wider world. So it is no accident that care and attention is everywhere being given to identifying and meeting users' needs, providing comfortable and well appointed research facilities conveniently linked to associated public amenities, and clearly demarcating them from areas of the building where, for their own good (health and safety) as well as that of the records (security, environmental control), the public should not venture. In this study, however, the care of the archives themselves claims prior attention.

★

There is much more to be said about the planning and location of individual functions, but that is postponed to Chapter 9. This preliminary sketch has attempted to convey the essential nature of an archive building, and the issues which govern its very being. With this background we can explore the specific concerns of BS 5454, beginning with the quest for a suitable site.

1. Scottish Record Office newsletter 14 (1991), p.8.

2. Bell 1979, pp.85–89; Bell 1980, pp.345–6; Ratcliffe; Konya pp.20–23.

3. In the former Eastern bloc, standard designs for archive buildings began to evolve in the 1950s [Shepilova 1990, pp.2–4] In other countries, model briefs have been published [e.g. Duchein 1988 appendix 2].

4. Among works cited in the bibliography those by Bell 1979, Bell & Faye, Buchmann, Duchein 1988, Faye, Gondos and Konya may be particularly commended. Their respective influences on the present volume are readily and gratefully acknowledged.

Chapter 2
The site

Writing of archive buildings in 1964, Belda observed that 'only rarely has the suitability of the site for its purpose determined the choice, and most frequently considerations quite unrelated to sound archive practice are taken into account' [Belda p.21].

This has often proved true for British archive buildings in this period. 'We have had to adapt our ideas to a limited site which is the only site which has been offered to us,' wrote one county archivist in 1988. Choice has inevitably been constrained by the availability and cost of plots for development, by national and local planning policies, or by building and environmental regulations. All these are understandable and in some measure defensible considerations. In just a few cases, however, unsuitable sites have been chosen for other reasons: because the commissioning authority lacked a clear vision of the purposes of an archive building or the needs of its users, or because it acted quickly, without due consideration of the objectives. This is much harder to defend given the guidance which is now readily available.

The choice of a site can itself make a critical contribution to the wellbeing of the archives. Taking account of the Standard but also of practical problems arising in individual cases, the Commission's advice to those studying the suitability of a particular site has been on the following lines.

In order to isolate the building from all hazards in adjacent properties and give good all round access to the exterior, for maintenance and for the emergency services, a detached and self-contained property is to be preferred. The land itself should not be contaminated. It must be capable of bearing the weight of the building and its contents without subsidence. The surrounding land and adjacent properties should present no obvious risk of fire or explosion, flood or damp, excessive dust or atmospheric pollution or, where magnetic media are stored, electro-magnetic interference. The site should not be in an area notorious for vandalism or crime. Proximity to the fire and police stations is an advantage.

Figure 3 at the end of this chapter summarises the risks associated with the site.

For the benefit of staff and users the following additional points have had to be borne in mind: ease of access by public transport and by car, and also for delivery vehicles; proximity to the headquarters or other relevant offices of the governing authority; access to related services such as reference library, and local amenities such as shops, banks and restaurants; pleasant working environment and outlook; relative freedom from noise and distraction.

Failure to meet some of these criteria need not automatically rule a site out of consideration: even apparently unpromising sites have been turned to good advantage by the skill of architects and engineers, the worst inconveniences being mitigated by design or structural features, orientation, or the redoubling of protection against the perceived risks. Commonly a site meets some of the criteria very well, and others less so. Northamptonshire Record Office is on a good open site adjacent to the fire brigade, but well out of town. The county record office HQ at Worcester is in a similar location, on a green-field site on the outskirts of the city right beside the new county hall, readily accessible from the M5 and served by buses, but distant from shops and other amenities apart from a natural heritage centre nearby which fortunately has refreshment facilities.

The Church of England Record Centre was relocated from Westminster to relatively cheap accommodation in Bermondsey. The move led to a sharp decline in the number of readers. Fears of a similar result from a move to a 'rather obscure location' by Suffolk Record Office (Bury) proved unfounded.[1] The archivist of an otherwise good repository in a run-down inner-city area reported in 1991 that the building was scarcely on the map as far as the local authority was concerned: out of sight and out of mind.

There have been several direct confrontations with the elements, particularly water and fire. Sheffield Archives is built astride a river. Borders Region Archive and the Public Record Office at Kew are situated next to rivers with a known history of flooding. In the later case a careful appraisal of the risks was conducted using theoretical models. Construction of the Thames barrier should have further reduced any risks, but as an added precaution the 'podium' is several feet above ground level and storage of records restricted to upper floors. Even the more extreme risks of fire and explosion have haunted a few sites. More than one repository in a converted building has had to drain garage fuel tanks on the site before occupancy. One local authority settled for a building within whose walls was an electricity sub-station serving not just the building but the district. The PRO at Kew is situated almost under the flight path of Heathrow airport.

Town-centre sites, despite their obvious convenience for users, tend to be more expensive than green-field or suburban plots. But this is not always true: Cheshire Record Office found that it was cheaper to convert a city-centre site than put up a new building in the suburbs. Tyne and Wear Record Office is only a few minutes' walk from Newcastle Central Station and yet its storage costs are low.

Some branch offices have been deliberately placed in libraries to bring together the archives and other local studies resources, as at Barnstaple, Lowestoft and Sevenoaks, which clearly influences the kind of site that can be used.[2] Other branches, as at Berwick and Colchester, are not linked to libraries.

Impact on the environment

The relationship with the surrounding environment is a two-way concern: not only the effect that the surroundings will have on the archives, but also the effect that the archive building, or indeed any building on the site,

2 West Sussex Record Office.

will have on the environment. Repositories with substantial storage capacity can bulk rather large in the landscape. If on top of that their predominant characteristic is unalleviated, featureless walls redolent of an industrial warehouse, they can be unwelcome newcomers, for example to an otherwise residential neighbourhood. The aesthetic impact of archival buildings is a matter for consideration at the planning stage.

And yet, an archive building can enhance rather than detract from its surroundings, and can serve a strategic purpose in a given neighbourhood. Sheffield Archives, for example, was deliberately sited in an area designated for 'cultural industries' by the planning authority. And almost irrespective of location, landscaping (where practicable) with lawns, trees and shrubs has become increasingly popular as a means of improving the appearance of a site and softening the impact of an otherwise austere building upon the local environment. Small gardens in internal courtyards (Northamptonshire), tree-lined patios (Suffolk:Ipswich), or just potted shrubs and flowers (Cheshire) have all found their place, and have cheered up the working environment for all concerned. The cost of gardening and other subsequent maintenance has, however, to be taken into account.

The 1990 White Paper on the Environment started from the premise that any building activity can have complex effects. Builders, planners and managers were encouraged to conduct environmental audits to assess whether the effects would be positive, negative or neutral on the atmosphere, the habitat (of humans, flora and fauna), and the heritage.[3]

Many authorities planning archive buildings were already taking these matters seriously even before the White Paper. On historic sites, for example, archaeologists have been called in to undertake excavations before work began. At Barnstaple, on a site beside the castle [see Figure 2], an excavation found evidence of pottery kilns of medieval and Stuart date. At Dorchester, Birmingham University

Archaeological Unit was called in. Excavations prior to building the extension at Lambeth Palace Library unearthed a 14th-century carved head of a king, perhaps from the

3   Medieval head from excavations at Lambeth Palace Library. Andy Chopping, Museum of London.

Figure 2   Site map of North Devon Record Office, Barnstaple.

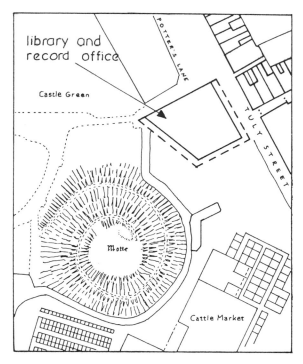

medieval great hall. Similar precautions have been necessary before a proposed extension to York Minster Library which is on a site close to the Roman forum. Nor has the wildlife habitat been entirely neglected: a survey of the site for the PRO at Kew in the 1970s discovered a colony of rare snails which had to be rescued and moved to a corner away from the building operation.

★

So for a variety of reasons the choice of site really does matter, and deserves careful thought. It has implications for much of the overall strategy on such matters as security,

fire prevention and environmental control which are separately treated below, and it is one of the determinants of the kind of building that can or should emerge from the planning process.

1. Suffolk Record Office Newsletter, January 1992.

2. Libraries themselves are moving into shopping and information centres in order to serve a wider population: Harrison 1990, p.ix.

3. An environmental statement has to accompany most planning applications, to meet the Town and Country Planning Regulations and EEC Directive 85/337.

Figure 3   Summary of risks associated with the site.

Risk	Possible counter-indicators
Restricted site	Building joined on to adjacent property Building shared with other occupants Insufficient space for expansion Difficult access for fire brigade
Subsidence	Adverse report by structural engineer Settlement cracks in existing building on site
Structural damage/ heavy maintenance	Site exposed to strong wind, strong sun, sea air Age of building Method of construction
Fire and explosion	Adjacent woodland, airport, military site, industrial premises, flammable stores including petrol tanks Appreciable distance from fire brigade
Flood and damp	Waterside sites, low lying ground, ground sloping steeply towards or beside site Necessity to use basement for storage
Dust and atmospheric pollution	Site adjacent to or down-wind of industrial processes, derelict or demolition sites, busy main roads, railway lines
Noise	Aircraft, traffic, industrial processes
Vandalism & crime	Isolated or partially concealed site Area known to be prone to vandalism or crime Adjacent waste ground as source of projectiles Appreciable distance from police station or security centre

Chapter 3
Structure and materials: general considerations

What sort of attributes or qualities do we expect of the structure of an archive building today, and what implications do they have for the choice of materials for its construction and fitting out?

It all comes back to the principles set out in the first chapter. Provided that everything about the building promotes their wellbeing, archives will outlive their present owners, custodians and readers, and with any luck their present accommodation as well. And the aim is nothing less than that.

First of all the structure must be resistant to fire, and as secure as possible against unauthorised entry. On both these counts there is more to be said than concerns structure alone, and what might be termed the non-structural aspects of the subjects are covered in separate chapters below. Apart from these prime considerations we could do worse than adapt a set of attributes or 'conditions' which Bruce Allsopp suggested might reasonably be looked for by the occupier of any building: that it should be (1) structurally stable, (2) weatherproof and (3) a means of '[moderating] the climate for the comfort of people'; that it should achieve this (4) with low expenditure of energy, and (5) with economy in the use of scarce materials; and (6) should combine durability with low maintenance costs. [Allsopp p.53]. In the case of an archive building this vision must be interpreted first from the point of view of the records, and only secondly from that of the people who use and care for them.

It is worth looking at each of these general attributes in turn.

★

Fire resistance

The 1977 edition of BS 5454 recommended that all materials used in walls, doors, floors and ceilings of the storage area should offer four-hour fire resistance, and this specific target is still retained in the Guidelines of the inspecting bodies even though it slipped out of the 1989 revision of BS 5454 in the final editorial stages. In a repository which takes account of all the Standard's other recommendations, of course, the likelihood of a fire taking hold for any long period, even out of office hours, is extremely remote. But fireproofing is important in both new and converted buildings, and a high standard has been attained in most of the buildings studied. In new buildings, compliance with the general building regulations is of course the first necessary step in fire prevention, but is not sufficient in itself, nor does it convey immunity from risk [Shields & Silcock p.167].

Brick, stone and reinforced concrete are therefore the predominant materials used in the construction of storage areas (as required by the inspecting authorities), and indeed for whole archive buildings. Steel and other metals liable to conduct heat throughout the structure in the event of a serious fire are of course used, but with some caution. In new buildings, timber and other combustible materials, including flammable finishes and fixtures, have generally been kept to a minimum in accordance with BS 5454. Where economy or the choice of a converted building has demanded the use of less than ideal materials, or where it has proved impossible for practical, financial or aesthetic reasons to meet the four-hour target in converted buildings, the Commission's advice has been to redouble

4 *Cheshire Record Office, showing the building's steel frame.*

other precautions and install at a minimum automatic fire-alarms linked to the brigade, and preferably also an automatic fire-extinction system.

At Cheshire Record Office, for example, a new steel frame and columns, on concrete foundations, were installed in place of the original timber frame, and a halon automatic fire-extinction system was added for good measure. The London Hospital archives centre, situated in the basement of a converted church, improved both its fire resistance and thermal insulation by spraying on to the ceiling a 30 mm coating of lympet mineral fibre.

BS 5454 further draws attention to the need, in the event of a fire, to exclude air which could sustain combustion. To prevent the spread of both smoke and fire, new repositories with air-conditioning are mostly equipped with self-closing ducts, vents and fire doors [BS 5454 s.6.8.2]. In this context, too, the siting and number of doors, windows, corridors, stairwells and lifts is important. Lift shafts are as good as chimneys for providing a through draught. This, in addition to security, is a reason why lifts should not be designed to open directly into storage areas. On the other hand, a sturdy lift is an asset not to be lightly spurned, and a number of repositories situated in converted warehouses, as at Bristol, have preferred to live with the problem but to provide additional protection: encasing the lift shaft within fire-resistant walls, and equipping it with special fire doors. The PRO at Kew has other vertical openings through its repository areas: a glazed light-well for which special research was carried out to check the fire resistance of the glass, and a 'paternoster' document conveyor which, like the air-conditioning ducts, is fitted with fusible links to shut it down in an emergency.[1] The huge repository floors can be subdivided into smaller compartments by emergency fire-doors.

Small compartments are easier to isolate in the event of fire and have long been advocated for library stacks as well as archives.[2] They might also make a gas-based fire-extinction system a cost-effective option. They are less necessary where a water-sprinkler system is installed. Compartmentation has other implications besides fire resistance which are considered in the next chapter.

Security

After fire-resistance, security looms especially large in any consideration of structure and materials. In both new and converted archive buildings special attention is being paid to the dimensions and materials of all openings in the shell: doors, windows, vents, chimneys, inspection hatches, etc., and to external features such as window ledges, buttresses, drainpipes and fire-escape ladders, all of which might assist climbing to upper levels, afford concealment, or invite unauthorised entry.

One repository with an internal courtyard invisible from the street added anti-climb paint to the courtyard drainpipes, and alarms to the windows overlooking the courtyard, even at high levels. Another, requiring a fire-escape ladder from a first-floor strongroom, chose a type which is openable from its folded position only at the point of escape at the top. Many purpose-built repositories have been designed with drainpipes beyond the reach of windows, or recessed within small buttresses to make them almost impossible to climb.

In the United Kingdom, archive buildings are no longer being designed, as they were for a time following the second World War, with protection from the effects of outright war in mind, although in the private sector some archive storage firms such as Security Archives (in Eisenhower's wartime bunker below Goodge Street in London) have occupied underground premises that were already bomb-proof. For different reasons (to guard against the risk of fire or explosion) the National Film Archive uses another bunker, in the country, for storing its stock of cellulose nitrate film. Terrorist bomb or incendiary attacks on public buildings, usually stopping short of their complete destruction, are however a present reality, and have been taken into account in the structure, design and security of some archive buildings including the Public Record Office at Kew and the new building now in progress there, and at Southampton University Library, where potential unrest by the student body was also a consideration. Among precautions at the Public Record Office of Northern Ireland, windows are fitted with anti-shatter film.

Where the repository is just one department of a parent museum or library, or where it has tenants or is itself a tenant with others of a larger building, a means has to be found of demarcating and controlling its territory. The governing authority then has to take particular care to see that none of the other tenancies is in any way detrimental to the archive service, and to make the tenants aware of the particular requirements of the repository as to security and protection from hazards such as fire, flood and noise.

Structural stability

Archives are surprisingly heavy. Averages are not specially helpful because the materials are very variable in size and mass, but according to one calculation [Duchein 1988, p.46] the average weight of a metre-run of documents is around 50 kg excluding the shelf, and for large volumes may reach 90 kg.

Northamptonshire Record Office calculated that an average metre-run of its records weighed 69 kg, and a nine-bay system a total of 3,747 kg.

Floor-loadings, at every level where archives are to be stored, and also in other rooms which are to house heavy equipment such as conservation presses, boilers or water tanks, have to take account of the stresses which will be exerted when the building is fully occupied. BS 5454 [s.4.2] recommends, for evenly distributed loads of static racking, a floor-loading of at least 11 kiloNewtons per square metre. Even static shelving units have been known to buckle under the weight of the records, and indeed one record office was replacing damaged shelves when visited for this survey. Mobile shelving uses storage space more efficiently, but thereby concentrates the load for a given floor area. So the Standard recommends that manufacturers be consulted on likely loads before it is installed. It has had to be ruled out in a number of converted buildings where either the foundations themselves or the structure (especially above ground-floor level) have proved too weak. Occasional problems have also been reported in purpose-buildings. For example, a small degree of settlement in the building at Hereford and Worcester Record Office HQ led to problems with the tracking of the mobile shelving, the units tending to close of their own volition if left unattended.

It is surely self-evident that strong foundations are among the first requisites of an archive building. In converted buildings which have not already been used for heavy storage the nature of the foundations has had to be tested. For new buildings much depends on the geology of the site. West Sussex Record Office required deep piled foundations and Suffolk Record Office (Ipswich), on soft ground 200 yards from a river, deep trench foundations. Special care was also necessary over the Cumbria Record Office at Barrow, built beside an underground watercourse. Hampshire's new building, on solid well drained chalk, had to have piled foundations to carry the weight of mobile racking. The PRO at Kew is built on a concrete raft sunk deep into the ground to allow for two basement floors, tanked because they are below the water table and on land adjacent to the Thames. Northamptonshire was more fortunate in finding a site where the repository could be built on solid bedrock.

Weatherproofing and environmental control

The shell of an archive building serves to buffer the contents against all external forces: lightning and tempest, of course – and at least one new record office, at Lichfield, has been struck by lightning – but also the regular forces of rain and wind, heat and cold, and daily variations in relative humidity.

Air-conditioning, separately considered below, can be a valuable asset. But other countries which experience greater extremes of heat and cold than the United Kingdom and yet lack the resources to consider air-conditioning have long known how to live comfortably without it, relying instead on buildings of substantial mass to buffer the internal against the external environment, and developing other design features such as overhanging roofs to shade and shelter the walls, or minimal fenestration in walls which directly face a hot sun. Similar attributes in the thick, stone-built muniment rooms of an earlier era, have assisted the survival of medieval documents, again without recourse to any high-tech solutions.

High thermal inertia

Taking such precedents into account, and further motivated by the high cost of energy, German archivists undertook experiments in the 1960s to design a modern European archive repository in which temperature and relative humidity would be stabilised mainly by using materials of high thermal mass combined with generous insulation, and by encouraging natural ventilation through cavity walls. 'High thermal inertia', that is a slow or nil indoor response to changes in the outdoor environmental conditions, has since been branded the 'low-tech' solution to problems of archive storage, and may almost be said to have become the new orthodoxy through international discussion and the wide emulation of the technique. It is still looked on with scepticism by some British architects who tend to see air-conditioning as the only reliable means of controlling the storage environment. It was, for example, considered but rejected for Dorset Record Office and for the BBC Written Archives where cost was the determining factor.

The city archives in Cologne (1971) was among the first to claim to have achieved high thermal inertia, coupled with ventilation by natural means, without significant mechanical assistance [Stehkaemper; Thomas 1988]. As a result it was used as a model by those planning other European archives: the Algemeen Rijksarchief (The Hague), the Bundesarchiv (Koblenz), and other buildings in Germany, Austria and Switzerland.

At Koblenz, behind the windowless granite outer wall of each strongroom there is a cavity 8 cm deep, which continues up to, and along under the roof; next comes a 6 cm layer of insulation, followed by a plastic membrane to exclude any condensation, and finally a brick wall 49 cm thick.[3] As a further defence, the outer wall of the repository is not itself the outside wall of the building. Each of the hexagonal storage areas is surrounded by a corridor separating it from outside walls or from the next adjacent unit. Intake of external air is controlled by computer and limited to times when the external conditions sufficiently match the required parameters. For the remainder of the time, the existing air is recycled. On the coldest winter days some background heating is provided, and for a small number of days a year some dehumidification. A similar system, stopping short of full air-conditioning, but including ducting for its future installation if necessary, is planned for the Scottish Record Office's new building.

High thermal inertia was promoted in Britain in the 1989 revision of BS 5454 [s.7.2] and has now been implemented with apparent success – it is still early days to judge – in the county record offices of Suffolk (Ipswich) and Northamptonshire. Similar potential is evident also in a number of other repositories which have actually opted for full air-conditioning as their main defence (BBC Written Archives, Hampshire 1993, National Film Archive, West Sussex), and there is nothing to prevent the two concepts being employed side by side.

The repository block at Suffolk Record Office, Ipswich (architects Henk I Pieksma and Ms Jocelyn B Dalley) drew on the experience of Cologne and a number of other German and Dutch repositories.[4] Its concrete frame is encased in a double cavity brick wall. The outer wall, of dark red brick to blend in with the adjacent school buildings which form the remainder of the record office, is one brick (112 mm) thick, pierced at frequent intervals near its foot by air-bricks which allow air to be naturally drawn in to the first cavity (70 mm) and to rise by convection into the roof void. Next comes a layer of insulation in the form of 110 mm thermalite blocks, then a further but smaller cavity (25 mm) and then the main internal brick wall, which is 300 mm thick, finished on the interior with a 13 mm coating of plaster. Much the same techniques are continued in the roof void, where above the flat concrete slab of the upper strongroom there is a thick (50 mm) layer of insulation capped by mineral-coated glass-fibre roofing sheet. Above is a well ventilated roof space. Here, however, some mechanical assistance is occasionally employed, with fans to draw in cool air to counteract solar gain in the roof space itself. The outer, pitched roof overhangs the walls generously on all four sides of the building, sheltering them from heat and damp. This does not entirely eliminate solar gain in the upper of the two strongrooms, but appears to limit it very effectively to a few degrees centigrade even in the hottest of summers.

The technique has worked so well that for much of the time thermohygrograph readings are virtually straight horizontal lines well within the acceptable parameters of BS 5454 for both temperature and relative humidity (RH). They appear distinctly better than those published for Cologne. One consequence of dependence on such a design is that if temperature or RH do change for any reason, even slightly, it may take quite some time for equilibrium to be restored by natural means. With this in mind, both strongrooms at Ipswich are equipped with dehumidifiers mounted on the outer walls, with small outflow pipes descending through the cavity walls and then projecting outwards. In the winter, low-level heating is provided by means of a double row of welded water pipes mounted round the walls.

Unlike some of the continental models this building has no provision for mechanically-assisted internal ventilation and air circulation. Both strongrooms are fitted with tall, narrow, openable windows, nine on each of the longer walls. The windows are double-glazed in toughened glass and deeply recessed into the brickwork to minimise heat gain and loss and to reduce glare. It has proved more difficult than expected to use these to regulate temperature and ventilation without disturbing the internal RH by admitting the generally more humid air from outdoors. Ventilation and air circulation therefore rely to a large extent on the opening and closing of the strongroom doors and the turbulence caused by the movement of the large banks of mobile racking.

Some risks may perhaps attend this kind of operation, which in most respects has proved both economical and effective. In particular, there are no means of controlling or monitoring the indoor air quality or the volume of its through-put. Only time will tell how well the records stand up to the local air quality. But on present evidence Suffolk can be justly proud of its achievement, at relatively low cost and without recourse to high technology.

Similar techniques are employed in Northamptonshire, though in a repository of different design. There the architect (Graham Court; county archivist Rachel Watson) was able to use computer projections from Suffolk to assist his calculations. There are no windows in the storage areas. External air can be drawn in mechanically at a rate of up to three changes per hour if needed. Similarly, cooling air can be drawn by fans either through the cavity wall or up into the roof space. Low-level heating, when required, is by means of hot water pipes housed within the cavity wall. Portable dehumidifiers fine-tune the relative humidity. As in Suffolk, remarkably stable environmental conditions have been achieved with little mechanical intervention.

Success in employing this technique appears to hinge on the accuracy of calculations, for example of the thermal coefficients of each of the building and insulation materials employed, and of the effects of combining them in given ratios. Computer models exist to assist the calculations, but other factors of overall design including orientation and layout have to be taken into account.

Some architects and engineers aspiring to emulate high thermal inertia in this country, particularly in smaller premises adapted from other uses, have failed. Some have miscalculated to the extent that the repository environment continues to vary directly in line with external conditions. Some have indeed achieved a degree of environmental stability, but alas outside the recommended ranges, in which case mechanical assistance, or recourse to time-honoured methods such as opening windows, has become almost inevitable.

Drainage

Another environmental factor to be considered is drainage. In new buildings special attention has been paid to this, both outside and in, to reduce the risk of flooding from any source. The archive department of the Museum of Science and Industry in Manchester, which is unusual in being wholly accommodated in a basement, has been built on a subterranean platform raised above surrounding drainage channels. Elsewhere, basements or low-lying ground floors have been fitted (as at Lincolnshire, where they did not at first operate effectively) with one-way drainage valves to allow flood water to escape but not to rise, and with pumps for use in an emergency. Suffolk was not allowed to drain the surface water from its substantial repository roof into the adjacent street drains for fear of creating a flood there, and instead had to force its drainage down into shingle below adjacent playing fields. In order to carry rain water away from the roof as quickly as possible, Lincolnshire substantially increased the number of fall-pipes on its building.

Despite all precautions a number of minor floods have been reported, even in new buildings, almost entirely in public rather than storage areas, and arising from defective gutters and blocked drains, or from internal mishaps such as leaking kitchen pipes, or overflowing de-humidifiers. Where hazards have been predicted, precautions have been redoubled: floors, walls and ceilings have been tanked and flood-alarms installed.[5]

Energy

The brief for the new Hampshire Record Office specified that 'its operation must use as little as possible of the earth's depleting resources'. Although archive buildings have by no means been immune from the wider concern to reduce energy consumption, there remain many whose very concept is still energy-intensive: where, for example, air-conditioning has to be running continuously or lighting left on throughout the working day. While museums have been measuring their energy efficiency in cost per square metre of floor area, little comparable work has yet been done for archive buildings. Energy demands should be continually monitored and where possible reduced.[6]

But economy in energy consumption is another of those factors which cannot be considered in isolation from the overall environmental strategy. It is inappropriate, although not unknown, to make all doors and windows airtight without ensuring adequate mechanical ventilation, to design a completely windowless repository without making some provision for internal lighting, or rigorously to conserve or recycle heat to such an extent that the ambient temperature becomes too high or the intake of fresh air insufficient. An overall plan is essential.

Economy in the use of scarce materials

Current concern extends to all non-renewable resources including hard woods. The Department of the Environment has been encouraging builders, owners and occupiers to bear this in mind when conducting environmental audits of their workplace.

Low maintenance costs

Briefs for new archive buildings understandably tend to stress the importance of minimising maintenance problems. This applies both inside and outside. Inside, to assist with the overall preservation strategy, the building should be easy to clean. Outside, the challenge may be greater. In the course of this study the architect for Northamptonshire drew special attention to the durability of the materials, chosen to provide a building with a life-expectancy of at least a century. The main frame of the offices and public parts of the building is of steel, galvanised against condensation. For the repository block, concrete columns and beams provide additional strength. Engineering bricks promise a strong and lasting structure. In general, materials requiring only minimal maintenance have been selected, especially for the higher, less accessible parts of the exterior. The overhanging roof has the further benefit of protecting the upper parts of the walls from rain and damp.

At the time of construction or purchase attention is so sharply focused on the one-off capital costs and whether they fall within budget that planners are often forced into trimming what should have been essentials, only to pick up the bill another year as a maintenance cost. Worse still, this can lead to the indefinite postponement of solutions. It is much more difficult to put structural and mechanical problems right once the building has been occupied and the records moved in.

★

These attributes of an archive building have to be taken together as a package, and not seen as individual desirables from which a selection can be made as convenient. Strong foundations are of little value if the building has a weak roof which might render it unsuitable not only on grounds of weatherproofing, but also of environment, energy consumption, maintenance costs and security. Environmental stability achieved only by massive energy consumption also falls short of the ideal.

With these general considerations in mind we can now turn to look at some of the particular structural features of archive buildings that have required special attention.

1. See 'The Public Record Office, Kew: structural and mechanical solutions to the fire protection of irreplaceable documents', in *Fire Prevention*, 125 (June 1978), pp.16–19.

2. Cunningham 1968; p.412; Morris 1979, pp.10–11. In Europe, a common recommendation for archival buildings is a maximum compartment of 200 square metres.

3. Buchmann 1986, p.79. Corresponding measurements at The Hague are: exterior wall 10 cm, cavity 4 cm, insulation 6 cm, internal wall 22 cm.

4. The following section is based very largely on Jones 1990.

5. See the note 'Aqua Sentry at the Guildhall' in *Journal of the Society of Archivists*, 10 no 4 (1989), p.196. These alarms do, however, rely on water actually reaching the detector. Another system cuts off the water supply if there is a sudden surge suggesting a flood (Greater Manchester County Record Office).

6. The Energy Efficiency Office recommends a 'Normalised Performance Indicator' for this purpose. There are regional Energy Efficiency Officers in each of the Department of Trade and Industry's English regional offices, in the Welsh and Scottish Offices and the Northern Ireland Department of Economic Development.

Chapter 4
Structure and materials: particular features

Walls

It follows from what has already been said that walls forming part of the shell of the storage areas have to be sturdy, fire-resistant and well insulated. Reinforced concrete is the most commonly used material in the new buildings, but of course brick and in a few cases even some coarser, rustic building materials are not unknown in conversions.

Internal, rough wall surfaces have too often been left untreated, especially in storage areas out of public view. In the best examples, however, they have at the minimum been sealed: not for purely cosmetic reasons but because abrasive, usually alkaline dust can harm records of all kinds [Thomson 1986, p.133]. Some repositories have added a painted finish to cheer up bleak materials and enhance the working environment. Where archival materials are not boxed or otherwise wrapped, paint colours have to be chosen to limit glare and, where relevant, ultra-violet reflection. One possible disadvantage is that surfaces cannot easily be repainted once the records are installed.

In staff offices and public areas, a number of problems have been presented by the internal walls, ranging from the need to sound-proof one activity from another, through that of supporting the weight of book shelves and other fittings, to (perhaps the most challenging) the need to predict how the space might be used to best effect, or differently, now or in the future. Sliding partitions instead of permanent solid walls have been used, for example in the reception area at Northamptonshire Record Office and between the exhibition and education areas at Gwynedd (Caernarfon) to enable space to be used flexibly as required for meetings or exhibitions. At Hereford and Worcester (HQ) the search room and offices all have demountable partition walls to permit the subsequent adaptation of the space. In some smaller offices with a restricted number of staff (Barrow, Doncaster, Sevenoaks, Glasgow University Business Archives), and even in a few larger offices (Dorset), glazed panels have been inserted in at least one of the walls connecting the public search room to adjacent rooms to improve invigilation. This is not, however, recommended as the sole means of invigilation.

The role of compartmentation in limiting fire has already been touched on. But it has other practical consequences. A multiplicity of very small storage areas, like the old police or prison cells abandoned by Lincolnshire and North Yorkshire Record Offices in their recent moves, but still occupied elsewhere, can be an inefficient use of space on account of the number and positioning of the walls, and can make for awkward management. On the other hand, a moderate amount of compartmentation can make it easier to limit not only fire but also flood or infestation to one particular 'cell' without endangering holdings away from the source of the problem. Also, the environment in large undivided storage areas is difficult to monitor and regulate evenly, and this has been one of the factors frustrating efforts to rectify environmental problems in the PRO at Kew, discussed in chapter 7.

Floors and ceilings

Allowing for the requirements of floor-loading and fire-resistance, reinforced concrete is again the preferred material for floors in the storage areas of new buildings. Unprotected concrete screed, found particularly in converted warehouses and industrial buildings, may flake or break up with time and with the passage to and fro of trolleys.[1] Most repositories with this problem have sealed the floor, and/or covered it either with heavy-duty carpeting (in some cases carpet squares which can be individually replaced if they wear out unevenly) or with a washable, non-slip floor covering. Unscreeded rough concrete is entirely unsuitable, but screeding can be an extremely dusty and troublesome process if not undertaken before the racking is fitted (Strathclyde).

Care has to be taken to ensure that the materials are inert and unlikely to decompose to the detriment of the stored records. In conservation and reprographics workshops flooring materials must be resistant to spilt chemicals; and in special media stores and computer rooms where a build-up of static electricity from the wrong kind of floor covering could be harmful, special precautions have sometimes been taken, including earthing the racking.

In a number of new repositories (Northamptonshire, Hampshire) a raised floor has been installed above the concrete base in the storage areas to carry the mobile racking on a laser-adjustable mechanism to compensate for any settlement in the building.

Where the storage area in new buildings is of more than one storey, troughed concrete can provide strength to the upper floors without excessive mass (Caernarfon, Hereford and Worcester HQ, Northamptonshire). Suspended ceilings have often been introduced, to conceal the bare concrete slab or the trunking for an air-conditioning system, or (with insulation above) to reduce the volume of space to be heated, or simply to produce a storage area of more manageable size and shape (Doncaster). Whilst they may, on aesthetic grounds, seem an improvement on exposed raw materials, they can also conceal mishaps or design faults: rain water leaking through an air duct above the panelling, condensation, or even birds entering the roof space through the eaves. In storage areas there is much to be said for leaving trunking and wiring exposed for

5 Installing a suspended ceiling, Doncaster Archives Department.

6 The roof void at Suffolk Record Office, Ipswich.

easy access (Hereford and Worcester HQ, Northamptonshire, Sheffield).

Columns and supports

BS 5454 [s.4.7] recommends that internal structural supports for the building be kept to a minimum. They are the bane of the archivist's life. In the repository they limit the free use of storage space. Inconvenience can be reduced where, as at the BBC Written Archives, the building and shelving contractors work with the architect to plan the best use of space. In the search room, too, columns can be a problem if they obstruct sight-lines for invigilation, and the best designs have no such impediments.

Roof

A good roof may be the most critical of the frontiers between the indoor and outdoor climate, and recent experience emphasises the virtue in keeping the roof-line as simple as possible: a multiplicity of valley gutters and differential roof levels, particularly in older buildings, may lead to leaks and damp walls. A multi-gabled style has nonetheless been favoured by some architects for new buildings (BBC, Hampshire 1993).

Flat roofs can be just as much a source of worry, but modern materials may be coming to the rescue. Westminster's new building, at the planning stage during this survey, was to employ on its flat roof a Swiss polymeric waterproofing membrane which claims among other attributes to be resistant to damp, rot, puncture and tearing, as well as to fire and ultra-violet light, to be non-stretch and non-shrink, and to remain stable in a polluted environment. Time will tell.

At the time of its construction the roof of the Public Record Office at Kew (8,100 square metres) was the largest stainless steel roof in the United Kingdom [Public Record Office 1978, p. 125]. The top floor of the building is capped by a concrete roof covered with polystyrene insulation and felting. Above this is a space housing heating, ventilation and mechanical plant, and above that a timber deck covered in stainless steel to reflect sunlight and thus reduce solar gain.

Suffolk Record Office (Ipswich) similarly has a concrete slab above its repository block, topped with 50 mm of insulation and above that glass fibre and mineral roofing sheet bonded in bitumen. Here, however, in the absence of air-conditioning, the space above is empty, and is critical to the building's ventilation and cooling system. The tiled outer roof is carried on steel beams which project well clear of the outer walls, giving a generous overhang. Northamptonshire has a steel-framed pitched roof with concrete tile finish. At Worcester the pitched roof of precast concrete is carried on steel lattice trusses with 50 mm insulation and a zinc covering. At Hampshire (1993) the roof, which is above staff and public areas, is of steel with a layer of insulation below and a thin covering of lead above. It is carried on a steel lattice exposed to the offices below. Special attention has had to be paid elsewhere in this ambitious design to the waterproofing of concrete terraces with bitumen, felt and tiling, to guard against leaks in the rooms below.

In converted buildings, a poor roof represents a bad bargain. As well as the inevitable leaks, problems have included weakened security through skylight windows or the use of fragile materials (one record office visited for this study bore signs 'Fragile roof: use crawling boards'), and also heat gain/loss and condensation owing to poor insulation or poor materials.

On security grounds, roofs should not offer any unauthorised access to the building. Even at this level, inspection hatches, gallery windows, and vents large enough to admit humans should be protected by the intruder-alarm system.

Windows

Glass is fashionable as a building material, but has limitations in an archive building, particularly if the shape, size and style of windows offers any threat: to the internal environment (through solar gain, heat loss, condensation, admittance of ultra-violet light); to security (breakage and unauthorised entry); or (in the case of openable windows) through admittance of insects, dust and pollutants, and a flow of air to sustain combustion in the event of a fire.

There are rival opinions as to whether there should be windows in storage areas, and if so whether they should be openable. BS 5454 [s.5.3.4] favours windowless repositories. Following its precepts, a number of purpose-built archive buildings have completely foregone windows for their storage areas (Barrow, Lancashire, Northamptonshire, West Sussex), whilst in some conversions (Cheshire, Doncaster, Dudley) existing windows have been filled in. Greater London Record Office compromised by filling in to the top-most pane.

On the other hand the admittance of some natural light, even in storage areas, offers advantages: potentially reducing energy demands, and providing a less claustrophobic working environment. BS 5454 [s.5.3.4] acknowledges this, but recommends that where repositories do have windows they should be small, unopenable, barred and of strengthened glass, opaque if so desired, double-glazed and screened against ultra-violet light. The PRO at Kew has shallow horizontal windows in the top of each wall of the storage areas. They admit very little daylight and are not openable. The new Hampshire Record Office has small, unopenable windows in the repository.

As long ago as 1951 it was argued that 'no repository should be so constructed that ventilation by doors and windows could not be used' [Collis p.53]. This still deserves to be carefully pondered. It is an essential aspect of design at Suffolk (Ipswich) which has openable windows, deeply recessed into the walls and with a restricted tilt mechanism to prevent them opening sufficiently to admit intruders. They are not, however, fitted with mesh to exclude birds or insects. In case this is thought an excessive precaution, spare a thought for the archivist in another (converted) repository who was compelled to shoot dead a stray pigeon after several successive animal welfare agencies had proved unable to catch and remove it alive. This skill is not normally taught at archive training schools.

The use or non-use of windows depends on a number of inter-related factors such as the orientation of the building, the presence or absence of air-conditioning, and the extent to

7 Blocked-up windows, Doncaster Archives Department.

which the records are boxed and therefore protected against exposure. In France, where Duchein extols the 'germicidal' properties of sunlight, it is nevertheless recommended that no more than 10% of repository wall should consist of windows [Duchein 1988, p.144].

Elsewhere in the building the general concern is to minimise direct sunlight on records wherever they are being consulted or worked on. This can be achieved by orientation or other design features, or by screens, blinds and/or ultra-violet filters which may be integral to the glass (costly but effective and durable) or applied as a film to the surface (cheaper but needing periodic renewal).

In this as in so much else, low-tech solutions are often to be preferred. The designers of Hampshire's new record office, which includes extensive (already filtered) glazing in the public areas, contemplated computer-controlled blinds programmed to adjust to the sun's position whether or not it was shining. The proposal was rejected. Instead, staff are to determine when to pull the blinds. Supposedly automatic external blinds fitted on the British Library of Political and Economic Science in

the 1970s failed to perform effectively. In the new manuscripts reading room of the National Library of Wales, where natural light is provided from above through a glass pyramid, baffles have been installed below the skylight to deflect direct sunlight away from the study tables.

In areas set aside for reading microforms or consulting computer screens, more subdued light is helpful. Some have used completely windowless rooms for these purposes (PRO Chancery Lane, Suffolk); some have used low-level lighting controllable for example by dimmer switches, and screened windows (Dorset), others just a general location away from the windows or under a gallery (Hampshire, West Sussex).

Draught as well as light and security needs to be reckoned with when considering openable windows in public areas and offices. Those in the public rooms at Northamptonshire, for example, have been designed to minimise draughts which might blow papers around. They open at the top, or alternatively admit air through a tilting vent at sill level protected by a mesh. At Nottinghamshire the sash openings in the public areas are restricted to four inches.

Natural light is important to conservators, but direct sunlight is not welcome in workshops and exhibition areas. For conservation, a north or east light is best and natural light generally preferable to artificial. The workshop at Berkshire Record Office (purpose-built within county hall) regrettably has no windows at all. In sharp contrast, that at the Greater London Record Office (a converted printing works) occupies a long rectangular room where one wall is almost continuously fenestrated from bench to ceiling height. In Northamptonshire natural light from a skylight, but with no vertical windows, has been found inadequate. In Dorset, where the workshop faces south-west, its ten windows have been very effectively screened against ultra-violet, coated to prevent solar gain, and fitted with controllable blinds.

Except in limited contexts such as plant and reprographics workshops, windowless rooms make for an inconvenient working environment. The quality of life is unquestionably enhanced by windows offering a visual point of reference outside the room, still more if the view itself is inspiring (over the Dee at Cheshire, towards the city wall at Chichester, across the Menai Strait at Caernarfon). Offices with no outlook, especially where they are tucked away in the centre of a building far from natural light, or worse still wholly enclosed with no windows (Berkshire, parts of the PRO at Kew) are poorly appointed. Light can sometimes be shared, and a less claustrophobic effect created, by the judicious use of glazed panels instead of solid walls (Cornwall, North Devon).

Easily reachable and vulnerable windows, especially at ground and first floor levels, may need to be barred, to prevent break-in or vandalism, with the bars firmly set into masonry. Thin wire mesh alone is not adequate, although it may be a useful additional defence against vandalism. Other security implications of windows are separately discussed in chapter 5.

Doors

Again for security reasons, in an archive building the number of entries and exits for public, staff and records is preferably kept to the minimum necessary for compliance with fire and safety regulations on the one hand and efficient management on the other. Certain converted buildings have been found over-endowed with doors, some of which have had to be blocked up or protected round the clock by the intruder-alarm system. In the best designed purpose-buildings the number of doors openable from the outside is deliberately restricted, indeed preferably kept to a single one as at Northamptonshire, and there is no direct access from the outdoors into a storage area. Conversely fire-escape doors opening directly from a strongroom to the outside are made openable only from the inside.

On security and environmental grounds, outer doors ought to be weatherproof, air-tight, strong and fire-resistant. Conventional domestic or office doors inherited in buildings for conversion have not been adequate, and here and there even purpose-built doors have not proved equal to the prevailing weather conditions. Further problems occur if there are gaps below or around the doors, through which dust, insects, or the elements – including of course un-treated air – can enter the repository. In the case of glazed doors or panels, including also extensively glazed external walkways and linking corridors, special attention is required to the strength of the materials. Additional defences can of course be provided, as at the Post Office Archives where the public entrance and search room windows are fitted with steel roller blinds which are dropped when the building is unoccupied.

In order to conform with security and fire-resistance requirements internal doors forming part of the shell of the storage areas are normally of solid metal or thick wood (or a combination of the two). The width of all internal doors has to allow for the transit of trolleys loaded with records, and the movement of individual large documents or furniture around the building. At West Sussex and Northamptonshire some of the internal doors sneck on to a narrow, hinged panel which can itself be opened to increase the total width of the aperture when required. By contrast in one repository the largest map can only reach the search room by being taken outside through a fire door and back in through a window!

Overall shape[2]

In order to maximise the use of space there is a strong presumption in favour of square or rectangular rooms for all or most of the functions within an archive building. This offers greatest flexibility in planning the racking for both records and reference works, and the seating in search rooms, where rectangular tables offer best support to the materials being studied. It also applies in conservation workshops and reprographics facilities, to accommodate equipment and allow plenty of flat wall-space for display and mounting. Curved, acute-angled or multangular rooms and buildings may seem more eye-catching, but experience from converted buildings with such features suggests that they generally result in wasted space and an inconvenient working environment.

The nature of the site and the lie of the land may not be propitious for a building that is itself strictly square or rectangular, but this is not essential if the individual functions can be so shaped. Many different solutions have been found, some of which are illustrated in the plans in Part 2. There is no standard model.

In addition to the efficient use of the internal space, factors to be taken into account in planning shape will include:

- the cost-effective use of land

- the practicality of protecting the entire perimeter (which may argue against a low-rise building spread out over a wide area)

- the overall plan for insulating the storage areas from outside influences (which may, for example, call for their being cocooned in the centre of the building)

- the need to provide efficient communication, whether horizontally or vertically, between related functions

- power-dependency of the whole building (multi-storey buildings cannot function without lifts)

- the need to allow for eventual extension on the site (upward extension is rarely an option given the great stresses exerted by stored archives, and is usually only possible when planned from the outset)

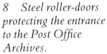

8 Steel roller-doors protecting the entrance to the Post Office Archives.

• planning and design constraints including the impact of the building on the neighbourhood.

A number of French provincial archives (Rouen with 33 storeys, Saône et Loire) have been housed in tower blocks. With the special exception of the House of Lords Record Office in the nineteenth-century Victoria Tower of the Palace of Westminster, the tallest archive building in the United Kingdom, when completed, will be the 6-storey tower under construction for Westminster City Archives Department.

1. See, for example, Strathclyde Regional Archives Report for 1986. The dangers are not, however, limited to concrete: Huntingdonshire has suffered dust from unstabilised ceilings and saw-dust infill between exposed floorboards.

2. See Duchein 1988, pp.171–3.

Chapter 5
Security against vandalism and theft

'Security', in the sense of the term now usually applied in manuals for archives, libraries and museums, is the protection of the holdings against *all* potential causes of stress, damage or loss. This is of the very essence of a 'repository'. The separate treatment given in BS 5454, and in the chapters of this book, to the choice of site and materials, the planning and design of the building, and protection against fire and adverse environmental conditions, is for convenience only. None of these can be considered in isolation without weakening the strategy. The present chapter, therefore, although confined mainly to protection against deliberate criminal acts, should be seen in that wider context.

The incidence of vandalism and theft

No comprehensive figures have been compiled on the incidence of vandalism and theft in the United Kingdom's record repositories, but enough individual cases have been reported to demonstrate a need for vigilance. Repositories are naturally reluctant to discuss their vulnerability or reveal the precise measures taken to prevent incidents. There is a strong case for withholding full details of the defences, including the exact location of detection and alarm devices, except perhaps in the public areas, where their visibility might prove a deterrent. Those repositories which allow public visits behind the scenes are having to take this into account.

Vandalism is currently a more widespread problem than theft, and was added to the list of hazards mentioned in the 1989 edition of BS 5454. In the case of archive buildings, vandalism appears to be random and opportunistic, and not targeted on archives for their own sake. What attracts is the opportunity presented by the building's location, features, structure and materials to satisfy the vandal's urges: large areas of uninterrupted wall ideal for graffiti, windows that make good targets for projectiles, flat roofs on which pranks can be performed (including one reported case of a barbecue being held), shrubs which can be hacked down, and so on. Shortly before it was visited in preparation for this study, one repository situated on the weekly migration path of football crowds, and with semi-derelict land to the rear used as a car park and providing a ready supply of projectiles, had had a window damaged. Another record office has told successively in its annual reports for 1981–2, 1983–4, 1985–6 and 1988 of recurring bouts of petty vandalism.

Vandalism may merge into more serious crime such as arson or the theft of lead or other roofing materials. American research warns of revenge attacks on libraries by disenchanted members of staff. This does not seem to be a problem among archive buildings in this country. But in view of the high percentage of general fires now attributed to arson, and their incidence in certain types of building, including notably schools, those contemplating converted buildings will wish to take appropriate precautions. One repository housed in a former school had the lead stolen from its roof. Its loss was not apparent until the walls and ceilings of its search room and offices began to show signs of extreme damp.

On the whole, archive buildings are not promising places for random or speculative thefts involving break-ins. Few other than initiates – staff and readers – have any idea what they contain, let alone its value. There are exceptions in the case of national repositories and university libraries where individual items, and their value, might be well publicised. Archive strongrooms are doubly unpromising because even a thief who knows roughly what they contain will need to penetrate certain physical barriers and unknown degrees of security to reach them, and then need to know what is where, among anonymous-looking storage boxes. Any overview of security strategy must take account of the risk of theft by a member of the staff.

No British repository has reported any break-in in this period motivated by the desire to steal records. Unfortunately, thefts without break-ins have proved all too easy during normal opening hours. Although making the records available for public inspection might be thought almost as central as security to the concept of the record repository, this more than any other single factor is what exposes them to risk. When they are removed from their safe storage for inspection in the search room their nature and content, perhaps known only dimly up to that point from a description in a finding-aid, become apparent to the reader. For a while the baton of custodial trust changes hands. It is the price most owners and custodians willingly pay to share our written heritage as widely as possible. Very occasionally that trust has been broken.

Most known thefts of records in this country seem to have been motivated by a desire to possess particular kinds of documents – or parts of documents, such as maps, stamps and autographs – or to make money by selling them. Other potential motives might include the wish to tamper with the evidence. A few breaches of security have hit national headlines in the period, demonstrating the continuing vulnerability of archival material and, for the curator, the perils of relaxing vigilance or settling for half-measures in security.

One thief arrested and tried in 1986 was sentenced to 18 months imprisonment for stealing from many repositories several thousand individual documents of postal history interest. This case, which attracted wide publicity,

prompted earnest discussion in the profession about security measures, and many improvements have been introduced as a result. The costs of tighter security have to be weighed against those of staff time in unscrambling the problems arising from stolen (and, just as pertinent, subsequently re-patriated) records on the one hand, and against the lost good will of owners on the other. In 1990 another thief squirrelled away from the Public Record Office at Kew, a few at a time, large quantities of air operations and combat records of the First and Second World Wars. The thief was arrested and many, but not all, were recovered. These are only the best known cases. Other thefts or suspected thefts have ranged from documents, books, microfiches and microfilm equipment from the public search rooms to computer and video equipment from staff offices.

How much security?

Manuals on security make the point that before embarking on specific security measures custodians should assess the nature and degree of the risks involved, so that the defences may be proportionate. This applies on two levels: first to the holdings themselves, where common sense might dictate that the most precious objects should receive the greatest degree of protection; but secondly to the various areas and functions of the building, some of which might by nature be less vulnerable or offer less potential reward to intruders.

As far as the holdings are concerned, archives can be viewed differently from museum exhibits. Some documents or collections are of such importance or sensitivity, or of such high monetary value, as to require special security measures. For this reason a number of repositories have set aside high security or 'safe' rooms, caged areas, or other zones to which access is controlled more strictly than to the rest of the repository. Rarer reference books may need similar protection: at Lincolnshire, for example, secure storage for these has been provided within the strongroom. But this must not lead to the thought that material of less value can be left to its own devices. Each item irrespective of its value is unique and irreplaceable. None that are worthy of permanent preservation should be left at risk as a result of weak security provision.

As for the buildings, it can perhaps be argued that greater round-the-clock security should apply to any rooms or areas in which records are housed than, for example, to general staff offices and public areas. And indeed this assumption underlies the planning and structure of most repositories. It is not necessary to set up defences worthy of Fort Knox for the contents of a cleaner's store cupboard. But on the other hand if intrusion into the public or staff areas is made unduly easy because security is pitched too low there is no knowing what damage may follow, even to the records.

When the then Minister for the Arts allocated the papers of the first Duke of Wellington, accepted for the nation in lieu of tax, to Southampton University Library in 1980, he made the allocation conditional – in accordance with the Commission's advice – upon the university's providing secure accommodation for the papers. The advice of the National Museums Security Adviser was obtained and a part of the library was specially converted to meet his recommendations. During the 1980s other important collections were added, including the Palmerston and Mountbatten papers. In 1985 when the construction of a new wing provided an opportunity for more ample archive storage and a new search room, the Security Adviser was again consulted. Few British archives have been subjected to such a comprehensive inspection. As a result, the entrance lobby to the search room is staffed by a library attendant. The door is kept locked until the reader's identity and *bona fides* have been established, and is locked again after entry. The premises are amply provided with several different types of intruder alarms which operate round the clock. The search room is invigilated by an archivist, who has a panic button to alert the security staff in the event of any incident; it is also scanned by closed-circuit television.

Although it is unusual to provide such comprehensive defences, a proper review of security is desirable in every archive building. Some security measures are inexpensive and can be achieved even by relatively low-tech means. Indeed, there is much to be said for simplicity. As one commentator puts it:

> The archivist who relies on common sense and ingenuity will have a more secure repository than the archivist who depends solely on sophisticated security equipment. [Walch 1977/80, pp.1–2]

Having said that, some of the essential yet affordable security measures are more to do with good management than with good buildings: control of public admissions; staff selection procedures, staff complement, duties and discipline; control of acquisitions and the means of issue and retrieval of documents; control of keys and so on. Additional security measures announced by the Public Record Office after its thefts[1] included an increase in the number of security staff, tighter restrictions on readers' coats and bags, the provision of photocopies on yellow instead of white paper to avoid confusion with original documents, and the introduction of a new system of surveillance by closed-circuit television. Elsewhere there has been a general upgrading of admissions requirements and the introduction of readers' tickets, with other measures varying from place to place but including restrictions on the number of items which may be handed to a reader at a time, stamping or marking the documents, weighing them as they enter and leave the search room, and so on.

These measures ought to be cost-effective since they focus specifically on the area of highest risk: the public search room. No security measures, however, should be thought undefeatable: an experienced and determined thief can find a way through most defences.

★

The perimeter

Good security begins at the perimeter, whether that is interpreted as the boundary of the grounds or the outer wall of the archive building. BS 5454 recommends [s.3.3] that a record repository should be demarcated from surrounding land by a perimeter fence. A physical barrier of this kind, if sufficiently high and robust, kept locked outside office hours, and not so opaque as to prevent anyone outside seeing what is taking place behind it, may deter criminals [Burke and Adeloye p.24]. That depends on the neighbourhood, and the likelihood of anyone being detected scaling the fence.

It may be both feasible and desirable on a new site to erect a fence. And some converted buildings, especially schools, come provided with one. But it has often proved impractical, for example in the context of a historic site, a building on a campus of other unfenced properties; a building directly beside a street or, as at Nottinghamshire, a canalside path, or where planners insist on an open–plan approach. In such cases the 'perimeter' has to be differently defined. But it is worth remembering that the absence of a fence has been known to increase exposure of the fabric to graffiti and vandalism and open up areas tempting for other purposes such as skate-boarding (Lancashire, Hereford & Worcester).

Whether or not a fence is provided, it is appropriate to examine the building and its surroundings with the local police Crime Prevention Officer and through the eyes of a potential vandal or thief. Will all of the exterior be visible from surrounding properties or streets? If some will be concealed from view, does that include possible points of entry, which will therefore require special protection? Is there anything in the structure or in the lie of the surrounding land or the landscaping which might offer cover or facilitate unauthorised access? (e.g. sloping land offering easy access to a low roof; trees or shrubs concealing doors or windows, or offering a means of scaling walls?)

Security lighting

Security lighting of the perimeter has been installed as an additional or alternative deterrent by a number of repositories: built in to the outer walls (Lancashire, Suffolk) or flood-lit from a distance (Nottinghamshire). Some have installed exterior closed-circuit television and/or video surveillance (Lancashire, PRO Kew).

Intruder alarms

Whilst it is possible to fit the fence, or any open area surrounding the building, with intruder-detectors, in practice most repositories have tended to concentrate their limited budgets on detecting either the actual penetration of the shell by the breaking of doors or windows, or the resulting invasion of internal space.

Some potential points of entry into the repository require intruder-alarms which operate round the clock. This is especially true of any external doors, loading bays etc which are not permanently visible to a member of staff, and fire doors or other exits intended for use only in an emergency. It is not necessary for a new building to be so designed that public routes, whether for general transit, access to WCs or even fire-escapes, pass through restricted areas. Occasionally in the case of adapted buildings this has proved unavoidable, and then additional security measures are necessary.

BS 5454 recommends that an intruder-alarm system be provided in accordance with BS 4737. The inspecting authorities further recommend that it be linked to a police station or security agency, a practice now widely adopted. An alarm bell alone, although it may drive off intruders, is not a satisfactory substitute. Some favour an alarm which alerts the security authorities without ringing a bell on the site, thus perhaps improving the chances of catching the intruder red-handed; the effectiveness of such a strategy depends very much on the likely speed of response to any call.

The choice of system, or combination of systems, suited to local needs is best discussed with the Crime Prevention Officer rather than directly with the alarm manufacturers, who may be concerned to sell a particular product. The various kinds of alarm available are described in detail in a number of manuals [Burke and Adeloye pp.42–54; Simonet 1990] but the technology is continually changing. Broadly they fall into two categories: those which detect the penetration of the building's shell and those which detect movement, sound or heat within. In repositories housing photographs, film and magnetic media special care has to be taken to ensure that beams or fields from the alarm equipment cannot pose any threat to the integrity of the stored media.

Both security- and fire-alarms can be extremely sensitive instruments. False security alerts have been caused in archive buildings by vibrations, noise or lights (even outside the building), lightning, air turbulence, twigs being blown against a window, a poster falling off a wall, and even the movement of water in fall-pipes. In one repository sonic alarms were triggered by the accidental dropping of a scaffolding pole by a workman refurbishing the building. Careful location and angling of the detectors can help, and to minimise the number of false alarms it may be advisable to increase the number and variety of sensors that have to be activated before the alarm sounds.

Locks

BS 5454 recommends [s.5.3.5.] that all doors giving access to the building from the outside, or to the storage areas from inside the building, should be fitted with mortice deadlocks or security bolts. Many repositories apply this degree of security even during the working day, but some of the larger and busier ones, where there is constant need for staff access to the storage areas, bar the way to an otherwise open storage area at these times by siting the entry to the storage area behind a staff point or counter and/or by using combination locks or pass cards similar to those in use in bank cash dispensers. Locks of this kind can be useful at other frontiers between the public and private parts of the building, and in order to control access to other floors where a lift is used. Attention has also widely been paid to the control of keys, and to the avoidance of exposed external door-hinges and pins.

Controlling public access

The period under review has seen major improvements in the design and control of the public areas in archive buildings, largely in response to the great increase in the number of public visits.

A clearly signed public entrance, at the same level as the search room, is a useful defence against a visitor wandering in through any other door (although none of these other points of entry should be left unlocked). A number of repositories control entry to the foyer/entrance lobby by means of an entry-phone (Church of England Records Centre; Northamptonshire; Glasgow University Business Records Centre). Where, alternatively, the outer door is left unlocked during office hours, admittance is normally either to a staffed reception area or to a hall or corridor from which the public route is unambiguous.

The main entrance can be a weak spot in the security of buildings converted from other uses if, as is often the case, it is a confluence of corridors from the different parts of the building, or of stairs or lift(s) giving access to all floors. Signs have a vital part to play inside as well as out, but unless the entrance is permanently staffed and it can be guaranteed that the staff's attention will not be diverted, physical barriers such as lockable doors and partitions may be needed to channel the public in the right direction.

There has also been a marked improvement in provision for the deposit of readers' coats and bags. Some medium-sized repositories, where an appreciable quantity of belongings may need to be deposited, have found it necessary to staff this facility. The most usual alternative is self-service lockers, now very widely instal-led. They are not required by all readers, which makes the calculation of their size and number somewhat arbitrary. They should not be situated within the search room itself unless they are on the outside of a security check-point which readers have to pass before re-claiming their bags.

Search room

The public search room is a high security area which ideally has only one point of public entry/exit (apart from any emergency exits), on which staff attention can be properly con-centrated. Cheshire and Lancashire Record Offices have introduced turnstiles, and several others have a security gate under the eye of a member of staff. Northamptonshire protects the entrance to its search room by a security door controlled from the adjacent staff coun-ter. In the largest repositories, where a single door may be impractical, special care has to be taken over invigilation.

The number and location of invigilation points in the search room naturally varies according to the size and shape of the room. Where there is a free choice in the design, a room of simple square or rectangular shape, but not too long and narrow, is preferable to one of irregular shape with alcoves or blind corners which make for difficult invigilation. The best de-signed search rooms have no pillars or col-umns to impede sight-lines (Dorset, North-amptonshire, Suffolk), or at least have readers' tables and chairs so placed that they are not hidden from view. The height and positioning of free-standing bookcases, filing cabinets and other furniture, especially where used to differentiate functions such as reference or microfilm areas, should also not block sight-lines.

There is no adequate substitute for human invigilation. All other security systems, such as closed-circuit television, convex mirrors and magnetic or radio-frequency strips on reference books, have to be regarded as only a second tier of defence. If carefully designed, small and medium-sized search rooms may be effectively invigilated from a single staff point. But with the increasing trend among larger services to define separate though linked areas for consultation of finding-aids, microfilm and original records respectively, even a single point sometimes has to be staffed by more than one person. A raised dais or platform can give a better view.

When studying plans for archive buildings the Commission has to bear in mind that no opportunity must be given to a thief to leave the search room, even temporarily, other than by the main entrance. Lifts and stairs should therefore not open directly into the search room – a regular problem in converted build-ings, and even in some libraries – nor should there be other public rooms such as WCs immediately accessible from the search room, unless they are beyond a security check point. Thieves have been known to take records into a WC or wash room and hide them about their person.[2]

Other public areas

Although generally less sensitive than the search room, all the other public areas of the building require some security protection. The most important general principle, already out-lined, is that the public, including contractors and anyone else not on the repository staff, should not be able to wander unaccompanied into any of the non-public areas, either accidentally or by design. Specific monitoring or invigilation is needed in any display area, especially if original records are exhibited, and in the latter case security should be no less stringent than in the search room.

1. Keeper's Report 1990 p.6; Readers' Bulletin 7, 1991.

2. In American libraries it has apparently been known for a thief to drop a book through an open window and collect it from the outside later [Boss p.41]. This problem has been reported in Britain too, although not in record offices.

Chapter 6
Fire prevention[1]

Protecting their holdings against fire has always been recognised as one of the most fundamental responsibilities of archive custodians. BS 5454 helped sharpen awareness of this responsibility, and is the foundation for all the advice given by the inspecting authorities. As a result, much less is now left to chance, and the track record of the United Kingdom's repositories has been excellent. That, however, necessarily makes the approach to this chapter more theoretical, because there is little case-law to draw on about the effectiveness of particular systems in the context of archives.

Recent evidence suggests that archives and records which are not in public custody are more at risk. On several recent occasions archivists have helped in the rescue-work after fires in private premises, as at Uppark house, Sussex (1989), the town gateway at Totnes, Devon (1990),[2] and the parish church of St Mary-at-Hill, London (1988). For their part, public custodians cannot afford to relax their vigilance where so many irreplaceable items are assembled under one roof. This is underlined by the handful of reports of minor fires in repositories during this period. They arose mainly from electrical faults or the overheating of equipment, and in at least one case from a discarded (illicit) cigarette in a waste bin. All (save one in an unprotected out-store) were extinguished without serious damage. One was a fire in a wall-mounted air-conditioning unit. It was effectively extinguished by an automatic carbon dioxide extinction system which caused no damage to documents but a lot of smoke and dirt. The gas cost £1,500 and proved difficult to extract afterwards. Potentially more serious was a fire in the (paper) filters of an air-heating system ill-advisedly sited actually within a record storage area, a legacy from previous owners in a converted warehouse. Here, the fire was attributed to freak over-heating when a power failure cut off fans which should have cooled the filters. It was confined to the machinery in question but the repository filled with smoke. In another repository, fire broke out in a parked motorised trolley.

Archives themselves are not a fire risk, with the exception of cellulose nitrate film which requires special storage conditions because it can ignite spontaneously at high temperatures [BS 5454 s.11.6]. On the other hand, virtually all archival media are combustible and must therefore be isolated from the risk, whether this arises from deliberate or negligent human action or the malfunctioning of machinery and equipment.

Most fires are preventable, but preparedness is proportional to the time spent in predicting how they might start. Archivists have been able to draw profitably on the advice of local Fire Officers, and many have apprised the brigade of the special nature of the building's contents and the need to use the minimum amount of water in any emergency.

The risk can be minimised by the choice of a suitable site; by appropriate building design, construction and fitting-out, including the use of fire-resistant materials; by care in the selection, installation and maintenance of plant and services; by the provision of equipment for fire detection and extinction; by general attention to security; and by good housekeeping and management.

At the planning stage the most important precaution is the prudent siting of functions and stores identified as potential sources of fire: plant for heating and air-conditioning; the mains electrical supply; facilities such as kitchens or canteens; and areas in which flammable substances including paint, and cleaning, reprographics and conservation materials are to be stored. Some of these are in any case subject to the Control of Substances Hazardous to Health regulations.

Most repositories have taken heed of BS 5454's recommendation that it should be possible to isolate electrical equipment out of office hours. Some power is needed even then, to serve air-conditioning equipment and the detection and alarm systems.

Detection and alarm
[BS 5454 ss.6.8.1, 6.9.1]

New repositories now almost invariably have alarms linked to the fire brigade, either directly or through an intermediate agent such as a security firm. Whether the building is staffed or deserted, whether it is protected by an automatic fire-extinction system or not, a reliable means of detecting a fire and actively raising the alarm is indispensable. An alarm that sounds only on the premises is not sufficient, except perhaps where the building is staffed and patrolled throughout the 24 hours.

Detectors

Several different kinds of detector are in use, designed for differing circumstances. They detect respectively heat, or rapid changes in temperature; smoke; or flame. Since their optimum siting varies with the height of the room, the pitch or angle of the ceiling and, in storage areas, the amount of vertical space above the racking [Shields and Silcock p.338], equipment inherited from a previous tenant in a converted building cannot be assumed to be effective in the new context without experiment.

As a safeguard against false alarms (which have been caused by a number of unexpected factors such as dust rising during building works, or heavy vapours rising from a conservation work-bench) it may be worth installing two different kinds of detector. St Helen's,

Worcester, for example, has both ionisation and optical smoke detectors.[3] In record storage areas ionisation detectors are particularly recommended [Thomas]. Advice on the kind best suited to local conditions is provided by Fire Officers.

Fire extinction

NOTE: Information given below is based on the experience of British repositories in the period, and on published manuals and guidance, and should not be quoted as a primary authority. The advice of the local Fire Officer should always take precedence.

Fires are extinguished principally by sharply reducing the temperature of the burning material, by cutting off the oxygen supply, or by interfering chemically with the process of combustion. There is no universal solution. Much depends on the size and nature of the areas to be protected, the extent of compartmentation, the height of the rooms and the racking.

The best all-round protection comes from fully automatic fire-extinction systems. These may be thought unnecessary where an archive building is staffed round the clock or where, as at Northamptonshire or the Post Office Archives, it is situated very close to a fire station. And some Fire Officers have argued that the risk of a fire taking hold in high density storage with little air to sustain combustion is minimal. But where no automatic system is installed all other precautions have to be redoubled, and an automatic detection and alarm system linked to the brigade assumes special importance.

Automatic systems

Automatic extinction systems are of three main kinds, based respectively on gas, foam or water. All are problematic, for different reasons explored below, but cannot on that account be dismissed.

(a) Gas
The 1977 edition of BS 5454 took the view that since water can cause extensive damage to

records the use of water sprinklers could not be recommended. As a result, most repositories with automatic systems have opted for gas-based systems employing carbon dioxide or halon. Opinions have been sharply revised since 1977, and the 1989 edition of BS 5454 does not rule out sprinklers. This may become of increasing importance because the roles respectively of carbon dioxide as a 'greenhouse' gas and halons as a danger to the ozone layer are being challenged on environmental grounds.

Carbon dioxide: Glamorgan is believed to have been the first local authority to install an automatic carbon dioxide system in its repository, in 1951.[4] Many have followed suit. The gas is not known to be toxic, nor to damage records or equipment, but it relies for its effectiveness on replacing the available oxygen, and so its use requires care on health and safety grounds since at this concentration human exposure could result in suffocation. In a well regulated system, with an alarm sounding to warn staff of the gas being deployed, there should be no such problems.

Halons[5] had come to be regarded as the safer option, and have been widely installed in automatic extinction systems in archive buildings. At Cheshire Record Office a test of the halon system in the new repository, once it had been filled with records, extinguished a fire in 7 seconds.[6]

But since the break-down of the atmosphere's ozone layer became a matter of public concern in recent years, halons have come to be regarded as non-'green'. A British Standard governs the fan-testing of halon equipment to ensure that gas does not escape during a test. An active quest is in progress for an equally effective but environmentally acceptable alternative. Meanwhile, there are internationally-agreed plans to ban the further production of halons. At the time of writing the latest advice from the Department of the Environment is that future supplies for systems already installed will depend upon obtaining gas that has been recovered from surrendered stock and equip-

ment. So the installation of new halon equipment, even assuming this is permitted, cannot be recommended. On this issue above all, the current advice of the local Fire Officer should be sought by those contemplating employing automatic systems in repositories now on the drawing board.

Halon has a potential disadvantage in an intense fire. It smothers the flame but does not necessarily reduce the heat sufficiently to rule out re-ignition once the gas is switched off or exhausted, or the doors are opened, increasing the supply of oxygen. Another difficulty is that bromine in halons has been known to react with the metal in the valves and cylinders of the equipment, allowing the gas to escape gradually, unsuspected by the user, with the result that cylinders have sometimes been

9 Halon gas cylinders, Walsall Archives Service.

found empty when checked. False alarms are not unknown: the halon system at Tyne and Wear Record Office was activated by a power failure, and that at Lichfield when the building was struck by lightning.

The plant for an automatic gas system takes up appreciable space, for which due allowance has to be made when planning. To operate effectively, gas systems require a fairly air-tight environment. Their use in naturally well ventilated areas and large open-plan offices and storage spaces is likely to be ineffective or prohibitively expensive. Where such systems are used, thought also has to be given to the means of eliminating the gas and cleansing and replenishing the air after any incident. Also, since the gas is released under pressure any loose papers may be scattered if the system is activated.

(b) Foam

A foam-based automatic extinction system operates by filling the affected area with high-expansion foam to deprive the fire of oxygen, relying on the sounding of an alarm to evacuate staff first. It is difficult to test in realistic conditions where, for example, there may be no available lighting, and on health and safety grounds cannot be recommended in an archive building. No British repository is at present known to employ such a system. The Public Record Office at Kew used to do so in its basement, although no records were stored there, but the system was removed after it was activated during a false alarm.

(c) Water[7]

And so, what of water? Has its time come? Fire Officers have long recommended water sprinkler systems to archivists [Cunningham p.415]. In the past decade or so, experts have come to challenge the opposition to water for a number of reasons [Shepilova 1992]. Compared with the gases and with foam, it is cheap and (in the case of larger fires) more effective as a means of extinction. It is environmentally friendly and non-toxic. Sprinkler technology has evolved to the point where water need not enter the pipes until sensors detect an incident,

and then need not be discharged until a liquid surrounding the sprinkler head has expanded in the heat, breaking its protective casing and triggering the flow. Some archivists have expressed anxiety that sprinklers may be activated by a false alarm and cause unnecessary damage. But the manufacturers say, and experience seems to confirm, that false alarms and failures are almost unknown. Special precautions have been taken in a number of repositories which have opted for sprinklers. In the Bundesarchiv in Koblenz, Germany, for example, water cannot enter the pipes until several independent sensors connected to a computer confirm that there is an emergency. Water is then discharged only from those sprinkler heads in the immediate vicinity of the fire. Damage can be further limited by ensuring that the records are boxed.[8]

The operation of sprinklers is said to be so effective that one head may have an effective range of up to 100 square feet, which means that in many cases a single activated head may be sufficient to put out a fire. To be effective sprinklers require a specified minimum clearance above the height of the racking, usually of at least half a metre. It has been pointed out that in the event of the brigade's attending to extinguish a conflagration with high-pressure hoses a great deal more water would be used, and more damage result.

Some difficulty arises over sprinklers in storage areas fitted with mobile racking, because the water has to be able to penetrate to the seat of any fire. This has led the PRO to reject them for its extension at Kew. In the new building of the National Archives, Washington DC, USA, the mobile stacks are computer-controlled so that out of hours or on the sounding of the alarm they set 4 to 7 inches apart to enable the sprinklers to operate effectively if needed [Stewart 1990, p.16]. The new Scottish Record Office building will have sprinklers, and the shelving units will be kept 30 mm apart by means of rubber stops. The Greater London Record Office inherited sprinklers in its main building from the former tenants and has retained them, but chose halon for its new building because the installation was considerably cheaper.

Whether or not a sprinkler system is used, provision should be made – though this has not always been remembered – for the evacuation of any water and smoke accumulating in the repository in the event of a fire. This is particularly important in basements, which (on those and other grounds) are not recommended for storage.

Hand-held extinguishers

Whether or not an automatic extinction system is provided, manual means of extinguishing small fires are required in accordance with BS 5454 and the advice of the Fire Officer. These are usually wall-mounted in order not to obstruct corridors and circulation space.

Public areas and corridors are most effectively protected by water hoses [BS 5454 s.6.9.4] and/or water-based (red) fire-extinguishers. These are effective for the commonest fires involving paper and wood, but must not be used on electrical fires or those involving flammable liquids and chemicals. Record storage areas and electrical equipment, however, are protected with carbon dioxide (black) or halon (green) fire extinguishers (but on the future of halon see above).

Dry powder (blue) extinguishers may be used in the case of electrical fires and those involving flammable liquids and gases, and are generally safe for use with paper and parchment but not newer media [Duchein p.101].

Fire blankets still have a role in certain parts of the building, particularly workshops and kitchens where naked flames may be expected.

Security, housekeeping and management

Other aspects of fire prevention which relate more particularly to good housekeeping and management are not a principal concern of this volume but may be briefly listed. A number of

them are covered in BS 5454 and in the chapter above on security. In particular:

- there should be no unauthorised admittance
- a No Smoking rule should be strictly enforced, with the possible exception of designated areas; visitors and contractors should be made aware of the rule
- no form of heating which includes a naked flame or element should be used in repository or offices
- combustible materials should not be placed on or beside heating services, in or adjacent to boiler rooms, beside fuse boxes, mains switches or electrical equipment
- combustible materials including waste paper etc but also the records themselves should not be left on floors or in other places where they might become liable to combustion in the event of carelessness, eg in discarding a lighted cigarette
- flammable liquids should be stored away from sources of heat, in air-tight containers. Some may be liable to ignite spontaneously without exposure to any naked flame or spark
- regular inspections of the repository should be undertaken by the professional staff to ensure that the fire regulations are being observed
- all electrical equipment should be regularly tested
- regular fire drills should be held and good relations maintained with the fire brigade which should be given standing instructions on the nature and location of the building
- there should be a disaster recovery plan.

Fire-escapes

The first duty of the Fire Officer is to protect life, not records, and cases have been referred to the Commission by anxious custodians where the Fire Officer has insisted on a strong-room being used as an escape route. This should never be necessary in a purpose-designed building. Where, in a conversion or extension, it has proved unavoidable, additional security measures have been taken, including the use of alarms to detect the unauthorised opening of strong room and fire-escape doors. Fire-escape doors from the storage areas are, however, often necessary for staff use, and are best designed to open only from the inside.

1.   Among the works on this subject referred to in the Bibliography, those by Cunningham, Thomas (both 1986 references), Stewart, and Shields and Silcock are particularly relevant. A new Unesco RAMP study by Shepilova 1992, which appeared as this volume was in the final editorial stages, is also recommended.

2.   See, for example, Devon Record Office newsletter, 6 Nov 1990, p6.

3.   On the tuning of detectors etc see Shields and Silcock, p.319 etc. For an explanation of ionisation detectors see Hirst p.341.

4.   Report of the Glamorgan Archivist 1974–81, p.1.

5.   The halons believed least toxic to humans, in small concentrations and for brief periods of exposure, and approved during this period for use in extinguishing fire, were halon 1211 (bromochlorodifluoromethane) used in hand-held extinguishers, and halon 1301 (bromotrifluoromethane, BTM) used in automatic systems. Held under pressure, these gases need only to replace between 5 and 6% of the air by volume to extinguish most fires [Morris, pp.81–5].

6.   See FI Dunn, 'The new Cheshire Record Office: a nineteenth-century warehouse', in Norton p.26.

7.   The assistance of Dr Wolf Buchmann of the Bundes-archiv, Koblenz, and Mr Brian Alan of the British Automatic Sprinkler Association Limited in the preparation of this section is acknowledged.

8.   A controlled experiment by the National Library of Scotland and the Scottish Record Office, involving playing a hose on shelves of unwanted volumes and boxed materials for several hours, demonstrated that damage to the text block of unboxed volumes and to the loose contents of boxes was relatively slight. I am grateful to Andrew Broom for this information. The National Library of Scotland has recently commissioned a sprinkler system [Lee]. See also Shepilova 1992, pp.17–19, which includes a discussion of different types of sprinkler system.

Chapter 7
Environmental control[1]

By the time of BS 5454's first appearance in 1977 there was already a good deal of scientific evidence about the effect of changes of temperature and relative humidity, of air pollution and air circulation, on the traditional archival materials, parchment and paper. The Standard drew on this evidence, as well as on the formative parallel work of Garry Thomson in the museums field, to formulate recommendations on the control of the indoor environment (or, as BS 5454's first edition called it, 'climate'). In all the most important respects these recommendations had sufficiently stood the test of time to be carried forward unamended into the 1989 edition, where additional advice was given in respect of newer media [s.11]. The Standard has been widely influential in determining the storage environment in the new archive buildings of this period.

The most significant development since 1977 has been building to achieve high thermal inertia, which is fully discussed in Chapter 3 above. Other notable developments have included an increasing trend for temperature and relative humidity (RH) to be controlled and monitored by computer (Southampton University Library, Dorset and Lancashire Record Offices), and the provision of distinct environmental controls for newer media, not only in specialist repositories like the J Paul Getty Jr Conservation Centre of the National Film Archive,[2] but also in general-purpose repositories (including Dorset, Greater Manchester, Hereford and Worcester HQ, Sheffield, West Sussex).

On the whole, however, environmental control is the aspect of archive buildings where most has been determined (or most left to chance) by budgetary constraints, and where adherence to BS 5454 has been at its most selective and pragmatic, particularly over the washing and filtration of incoming air. A question often put to the Commission in one form or another is 'How far short of the Standard's full recommendations can we safely stop?' There is no short or foolproof answer.

It is worth restating that the fundamental objective of an archive building is to protect the archives against the forces which will accelerate their deterioration or otherwise put them at risk. This notably requires control of temperature and relative humidity. It may also require control of ventilation and air circulation. The strictest control of all these variables, as recommended by BS 5454 (see Figure 4), and by the inspecting authorities' Guidelines, both of which emphasise that *constant* temperature and RH are as important as the range [Guidelines 6.1], can only be achieved by a mechanical full air-conditioning system – and, what is more, only by one that is functioning correctly.

Air-conditioning

'Partial air-conditioning' addresses only some of the desirable controls, for example heating, chilling, humidification or dehumidification and air-circulation or some combination of these, whilst 'full air-conditioning' controls in addition the volume and quality of air brought in.

Systems of both kinds are found in today's archive buildings. They are notoriously prone to breakdown and malfunction. Almost every air-conditioned repository studied has reported problems.[3] As an initial safeguard BS 5454 recommends controlled installation in accordance with British Standards [s.6.6.1], followed by rigorous monitoring, the provision of alarms to indicate malfunctioning, and if possible (rarely applied) duplicate plant for use in the event of a breakdown. It is easy to see why thermal inertia, despite its capital costs, can be an attractive alternative!

The first British archive building to be air-conditioned was the Victoria Tower of the House of Lords Record Office in the 1960s. Here, the thick walls of the tower already helped to keep the building cool, and no chilling plant was required. The system was designed to take in external air through silica gel driers to reduce its relative humidity (RH) to between 50 and 60%, and this was found a decisive ally in the fight against mould [Anon, 1962].

How much do we really know about the consequences of decisions to install or not to install air-conditioning? There is enough evidence – some of it experimental, but some of it daily before archivists' eyes – that paper and parchment suffer damage from prolonged exposure to heat and moisture, from excessive fluctuations of temperature and RH, from dirt and abrasive dust, and from acidity (which may be either intrinsic to the materials themselves or introduced in their storage environment, for example by migration from wooden shelving or packing materials or by absorption of pollutants from the surrounding air). It is easier to identify the damage than to be sure (a) which factor or combination of factors has caused it, (b) whether or not it is attributable to the present storage conditions, and (c) whether it is a short- or long-term problem. Some of the dilemmas facing archivists as a result of these uncertainties were spelt out by Elizabeth Stazicker in 1987 in an important but unanswered article in the *Journal of the Society of Archivists*. Because little experimental data has been gathered and published it is less than clear what difference it makes to forego air filtration or washing, or even ventilation, and concentrate on achieving stable temperature and RH (which because they are the most easily controllable and measurable are often seen as the most important variables to get right).

Figure 4 *Temperatures and relative humidities recommended by BS5454.*

Material	Temp.	RH	BS 5454 paragraph
Paper/parchment	constant in range 13–18°C	constant in range 55–65%	7.3.1
Little used paper	ditto	40%	7.3.1
Safety film	[see ISO 5466]		11.5.1
Silver-image prints	[see ISO 6051]		11.5.1
Silver-image plates	[see BS 5687]		11.5.1
Silver-gelatin microfilm	[see BS 1153]		11.6
Gramophone records	constant in range 10–21°C	constant in range 40–55%	11.7.1
Magnetic tape (exc. computer)	4–16°C	40–60% (polyester 35–45%)	11.8.1
Magnetic media (computer)	18–22°C	35–45%	11.9
Compromise general conditions where special conditions not achievable:	13–16°C	50–60%	7.3.2

Other criteria govern these recommendations, including adherence, where relevant, to manufacturers' instructions. This table is for guidance only: the full Standard should be consulted.

Three kinds of problem have been reported:

(i) *Getting the system balanced at the outset, to achieve the conditions recommended in BS 5454.* This should not be finalised until the racking has been installed [Walsh 1980, p.75], and the system will require some adjustment thereafter as the archives themselves deflect the air-flow and absorb or give out moisture. More substantial modification has sometimes been needed where a building was still drying out when the archives were moved in. As a measure of the problem, it was estimated that some 100 tons of water were used in building Suffolk Record Office, Ipswich. Perseverance is essential, as success cannot always be assured at the first attempt. When inspecting repositories, the Commission usually allows six months to elapse from the date of opening before drawing conclusions about the readings of temperature and RH.

(ii) *Getting the system to perform consistently thereafter.* This may be due to essential flaws in its specification. The special collections department of the British Library of Political and Economic Science was the only part of the building to be air-conditioned when it was first occupied; the system now requires the regular ingenuity of engineers to meet any of the required conditions. The equipment is not always to blame. Structural problems may lead to the absorption of moisture from the surrounding terrain or the loss or gain of heat through a poorly insulated roof. The sheer size of a large repository can also present problems: and BS 5454 recommends small compartments for the storage areas as an aid to a controlled environment. Attention may also need to be paid to the siting of the air intake, and the times or external conditions in which it operates, to ensure that none of these is itself detrimental to the internal environment. It has to be recalled that air-conditioning is only one part of the overall strategy, which covers also structure, design and materials.

(iii) *Getting the system to perform safely at all.* Problems have ranged from one report of a system throwing itself into reverse and extracting the air from a strongroom, to certain health hazards discussed below.

A repository designed to rely on air-conditioning may well remain dependent on it for 24 hours a day, seven days a week throughout the year. It is unsafe to assume without careful monitoring that the equipment can with impunity be switched off at the end of the working day or at weekends and public holidays, which has posed problems for repositories housed in part of a larger, shared building where the system is shut down at night.[4] But with continuous operation, the machinery is put under stress. It may cope with normal external conditions but prove incapable of handling prolonged extremes of weather: several systems, for example, gave up exhausted in the exceptionally hot summer of 1990, including that at the BBC Written Archives where a condenser broke; and elsewhere there were a number of reports of indoor repository temperatures exceeding 30°C. The blame may lie with an authority which has unduly trimmed its capital expenditure and installed a system which could never meet the recommendations of BS 5454. One repository constructed early in the period at first suffered damp and mould in the furthermost recesses of the strongroom because its air-conditioning system, trimmed down to satisfy budget cuts, was too small to serve the whole area.

Air-conditioning is expensive not only to install but also to maintain, and energy-intensive to run. And the custody of archives, like any other public activity, cannot be undertaken without stewardship of all the costs. But certain of these may constitute the 'bottom line', the price that has to be paid in order to preserve our heritage in good order, and without which we ought not to be entering into the activity in the first place because the amount of protection we can then give will fall too far short of what is required.

Outdoor climate and air quality[5]

There has been some debate on whether the United Kingdom's outdoor climate is such as to require *any* archive buildings to be fitted with full air-conditioning. No general absolution can be granted, because there are appreciable seasonal and regional variations in Britain's climate. Some westerly areas in particular experience outdoor RH well in excess of that recommended for archive storage. Summer days everywhere can be humid, and even on rather dry days RH can climb sharply overnight. Cold winter days, by contrast, may produce low RH.[6]

Air quality is similarly variable, and although we may take comfort from the improvement in sulphur dioxide levels resulting from the Clean Air Act and the change to burning less sulphurous North Sea gas [Hackney p.105], there is still localised (and sometimes more general) atmospheric pollution from industrial activity and traffic exhaust gases, especially ozone and the oxides of nitrogen.[7] This has been highlighted in recent years by the monitoring of air quality on the national television weather forecasts and publication of data on sulphur dioxide, nitrogen dioxide and ozone levels on Ceefax. The context is appropriate because pollution levels depend in part on the weather. Wind may cause pollution to travel far from its point of origin. Absence of wind, combined with strong sunlight, may cause fumes to break down into harmful pollutants. Rain, by contrast, may quickly absorb and disperse pollutant gases such as sulphur dioxide. Some pollutants may be less self-evident, like salt carried in acid droplets by winds from the sea [Thomson 1965, p.152].

Some localities may be fortunate enough to escape the worst exposure to pollutants – but how can we be sure? The British Geological Survey library and archives at Keyworth, Nottinghamshire, decided that air filtration was unnecessary on its green-field site. Tests carried out on site before the building of the county record office at Worcester suggested that pollution was negligible, at least at the time when the readings were taken, though this may be an important modifier. In some of our conurbations, or beside or down-wind of busy roads or industrial activity, greater vigilance may be called for, but nowhere can be regarded as immune from periodic hazards of this kind. In some countries it is compulsory for ambient pollution levels to be tested before an archive building is erected [Shepilova 1990, p.5]. In the United Kingdom there is no such regulation, but this is another field in which solid evidence, gathered systematically over an extended period, would be welcome. Meanwhile, archivists should seek to identify the risks associated with opening windows or air vents. If they know, or have strong reason to suspect, that the external air is polluted, air taken into the building should be filtered and/ or washed [Duchein p.110].

Full and regulated air-conditioning substantially protects records against pollution. Yet, with rare exceptions such as Lancashire Record Office's new storage block and Glasgow University's Business Records Centre, few of the repositories studied have sought to implement the BS 5454 recommendations on both filtering and washing. Filtering the air through activated charcoal [BS 5454 s.7.4.3] and washing it in plain or alkaline water [Thomson 1988, pp.133–5] should reduce most of the pollutants, including particulates and harmful gases, to insignificant levels.[8] Repositories which rely not on air-conditioning but on opened windows or unfiltered air vents for the supply of air, may be storing up problems, both from visible accumulations of dust and dirt and from invisible pollutant gases, whose effects may be noticeable only over a long period. Some comfort may, however, be drawn from evidence that storing archives in acid-free boxes buffers them against most of these pollutants,[9] and that the fabric of the buildings can also act as an absorbent, reducing the direct threat.

★

Poorly regulated equipment can cause more problems than it solves. Even some air-conditioned repositories, including the PRO at Kew and Berkshire Record Office (although these are by no means the only ones) have detected outbreaks of mould attributable to malfunctioning air-conditioning equipment. Since archival moulds have been shown to die off where the relative humidity is continuously below 65%, it follows that where fresh mould growth is detected RH has been exceeding that level. This is most likely to be (a) because the system itself is incorrectly regulated; (b) because the walls, roof or floor of the building are drawing in moisture from an outside source; or (c) because the treated air is not penetrating evenly to all parts of the storage. The problem has sometimes been very localised, near external walls or directly below the air-conditioning trunking. An even distribution of air may be specially difficult to achieve in large, irregularly-shaped or relatively open-plan storage areas, particularly where mobile racking is employed which, unless regularly opened and closed, may prevent the circulating air from penetrating. At Berkshire the problem was solved by introducing powerful though rather noisy fans, and mesh instead of solid end-panels for the racking.

There is some disagreement on the rate at which air should be changed within a repository. In most European countries the norm is half or one change per hour in storage areas, and up to 4 changes per hour in rooms where people will be working [Duchein pp.108–9; Faber and Kell p.351]. BS 5454, by contrast, recommends the remarkably high rate of six changes per hour, which may be more easily and affordably attainable in a small repository than in a large one. The air handling units in Nottinghamshire's new building, for example, one for each of the two floors and still to be fully tested in practice, have been selected to give six air changes per hour in an empty room, and about ten changes as the rooms are filled, with about 90% return air and 10% fresh air in accordance with BS 5454.

Unlike the recommended levels for relative humidity, the figure of six air changes is more a demonstration of the great weight placed on air change and air circulation in the battle against mould than a specific threshold below or above which certain things will happen. What seems clear is that if the local circum-

stances generate RH in excess of BS 5454's recommendations, and there is also inadequate air circulation even in isolated pockets, mould will flourish. In technical facilities such as reprographics workshops where chemicals are in regular use a high through-put of clean air is essential on health and safety grounds.

In view of the propensity of air-conditioning equipment to malfunction it is as well to have a secondary method of ventilation, such as openable windows or vents. Where mechanical ventilation has not been provided, hermetically sealed windows, or no windows at all, could be a mistake. Other sources of disturbance to the air in the strongroom can be taken into account on the credit side. Opening and closing the door and moving mobile racking can appreciably alter the through-put of air [Bell 1979, p.88]. They can, however, disturb other parameters also.

It is possible to some extent, by means of partial air-conditioning, or by installing several separate pieces of equipment, to control temperature and RH mechanically without recourse to full air-conditioning, but there are pitfalls. Humidifiers have to be rigorously maintained if they are not to breed harmful bacteria and other micro-organisms. Dehumidifiers, if they are not (as at Ipswich) wall-mounted with an external drain, need to be continually observed to ensure that they do not overflow. They cannot usually be safely left running unattended overnight, which may be just the time at which they are most needed. Electrostatic dust-precipitators give out ozone, a powerful corrosive agent which can break down cellulose and cause fading in materials, and must not be allowed into contact with the records [Thomson 1965, p.157]. The costs of maintaining and supervising numerous separate pieces of equipment need to be carefully evaluated before a full air-conditioning system is ruled out.

The importance of proper cleaning and maintenance of all air-conditioning equipment, whether full, partial or free-standing, has been reinforced by the identification during this period of a number of illnesses which can be caused by organisms thriving in the equipment. Among these the most feared is legionnaire's disease, potentially fatal, caused by the bacterium *legionella pneumophila* which has a penchant for heating and cooling systems but can escape in droplets into the atmosphere whence it invades the lungs. Fortunately, no case is known to have been associated with an archive building. Reports of incidents in other kinds of buildings have however tended to rouse the worst speculation and fears when *any* ailments related to the air-conditioning plant have been reported among staff or public using a repository.

Micro-organisms including bacteria and fungi can thrive in water which has not been sterilised, and some people may be specially allergic to 'humidifier fever' and related ailments.[10] Archivists have been alerted to the importance of draining, cleaning and disinfecting the equipment to remove all risk of infection. In hard-water areas humidifiers may also need very frequent servicing or replacement to combat scaling.

'Sick-building syndrome' is a catch-all term, spurned by some specialists, devised to explain recurring illness among staff or public in a particular building, when the cause appears to have something to do with the internal environment. Often it cannot be precisely pinned down. It seems that it may stem from either physical or psychological factors or perhaps a combination of the two. From the human point of view the availability of enough oxygen in the air supply is crucial, whether contrived by opening windows and air vents, or mechanically through an air intake system. Double-glazing, insulating doors and windows to prevent draughts, and blocking up old fire-places in the interests of energy conservation can all stoke up problems if thought has not been given to alternative sources of fresh air. Human occupancy leads naturally to a build-up of exhaust carbon dioxide which if not compensated for can cause stuffiness.

Air-conditioned buildings without openable windows appear more prone to complaints. Dusts, particulates and pollens may be carried through air-conditioning ducts and vents if the intake air is not properly filtered and the ducting itself kept clean. Smoke, and smells ranging from body odours to paints, chemicals and the gases given off by furnishings, furniture and insulation materials, can contribute to the problem. Excesses of heat, cold, dryness or draught are other common complaints.

Archive buildings cannot be thought immune from such problems. Attention therefore has to be paid to the adequacy of air circulation not just in the storage areas but throughout the building, and the extraction of carbon dioxide and pollutant gases. To some extent this can be measured scientifically. It has been shown that the human perception of 'freshness' is rather subjective and closely related to the temperature at which the individual feels most comfortable [Faber and Kell p.349; McIntyre p.279]. Cool, recycled air may be acceptable on a hot, stuffy day, but for much of the time people may prefer a gentle breeze through an open window, which incidentally puts them in touch with the external environment, an important psychological factor. But what quality of air are they breathing?

Ergonomic factors too affect one's view of, or allergy to, the workplace. The correct positioning of desks and tables in relation to walls, windows and workmates, the level and angle of artificial lighting or exposure to the glare of the sun, and the extent to which these can be controlled by blinds, the depth or narrowness of the field of vision and the nature of the view from the workplace – perhaps above all the extent to which one can control one's own working environment – all contribute to the overall well-being of the building's occupants, and to what might be called the 'well building syndrome'. It is the task first of planners and then of management to ensure that this is achieved and maintained.

The worst reported malfunction of air-conditioning equipment in British archives occurred at the Public Record Office, Kew, from 1984. Unacceptably high temperature and low relative humidity caused complaints of sickness among the staff, and led to several successive closures of the Office. An independent survey by consulting engineers found no evidence of serious hazard but inadequacies in the air-conditioning and air distribution system. Remedial work took longer than expected to complete, and some difficulties remain even at the time of writing, when a major overhaul of the system is about to begin.[11]

It must be concluded that risks attend all air-conditioning, that conditions must be rigorously monitored no matter what degree of mechanisation is relied on, and that the performance and maintenance of the equipment need to be thoroughly vetted.

Ideally the environmental conditions recommended in BS 5454 should be maintained everywhere in the building where records are being consulted or worked on, but (as with lighting) some compromise is inevitable for human comfort. Very few conservation workshops are yet provided with air-conditioning regulated for the good of the records, and in some repositories where the change of environments between strongroom and search room is considerable, remedial action has had to be taken, for example by providing humidifiers in the search room (North Yorkshire). In public areas, openable windows are a useful aid to ventilation, and have been provided even in some air-conditioned buildings (Dorset, Hampshire 1993). To improve ventilation quickly or for short periods without leaving windows open, extractor fans have been used at Dorset.

Archivists everywhere have taken very seriously the environmental recommendations of BS 5454. There remains a considerable agenda for further research and development on the nature and relative seriousness of the risks to archives from environmental factors.[12]

1. Among works cited in the Bibliography, attention is particularly drawn to BS 5454 section 7, and to Thomson, *The Museum Environment* (1986).

2. Research established high humidity to be a major factor in the decomposition of acetate film [British Film Institute annual report 1990–1, p.14], and efforts have been made to reduce progressively the RH of the storage.

3. Libraries have experienced the same problems [Harrison 1990, p.ix].

4. Where air-conditioning has been installed as an additional measure in a building which itself offers high thermal inertia, there may be a case for conducting controlled experiments to assess the effects on the internal environment of turning the system off from time to time. If little or no change in temperature and relative humidity results, economies may be possible.

5. On this topic see particularly Thomas 1988; Thomson 1965; and Thomson 1988, pp.130–58, 244–64.

6. The Meteorological Office publishes selected humidity statistics and a series of papers on the Climate of Great Britain, region by region.

7. The *Guardian* reported on 14 December 1991 the highest levels of nitrogen dioxide from car exhausts in London since records began in 1976, and that evening's television weather forecast recorded poor quality air and high levels of sulphur dioxide pollution.

8. Walsh gives specific recommendations on equipment; see also Duchein 1988, pp.110–11; Thomson 1965.

9. See the notes by WH Langwell in *Journal of the Society of Archivists*, I (1955–59), pp.291–3; and II (1960–64), pp.166, 221–2.

10. 'Humidifier fever' is manifested in generally mild, influenza-like symptoms (headache, fever, cough, breathlessness) which gradually pass off after the victim is removed from the contaminated environment.

11. For a fuller account see PRO Keepers' Reports, including the reports of the Advisory Council on Public Records, since 1984, and articles in the *Architects' Journal*, 179 no 13, p.33, and no 17, p.29 (1984), 'Problems at the PRO'.

12. A starting point might be the work of May Cassar and Tadj Oreszczyn on environmental surveys in museums. See *Museums Journal*, January 1992, p.36.

Appendix to Chapter 7

A note on lighting

Exposure to light, especially ultra-violet light, contributes to the ageing of most archival materials. Electric lighting, no less than natural light, has environmental implications within an archive building, and of course contributes to the expenditure of energy. A good deal of practical guidance is available, both in BS 5454 and in the text books, on such matters as lighting levels for storage and exhibition and for the consultation of records in the search room.

A number of energy-saving measures have been adopted in storage areas. These include banks of lights triggered by movement sensors when anyone enters a given aisle (PRO Kew, Greater London RO, Lincolnshire, National Film Archive), lighting brackets fitted to the top of mobile shelving which switch on and off automatically as an aisle is opened up (British Library of Political and Economic Science), lighting on timer switches at the end of each unit of mobile racking (Post Office Archives) and, the longest established method, pull-cord switches for use as required. It is helpful if all lights which have to be switched off out of hours can be controlled from a central point. Among problems reported, one or two repositories which have had lighting installed before racking have found the layout and intensity of the lighting inadequate to serve the actual layout of aisles and gangways.

Among the exhibition areas visited, Dorset has tracked spot-lighting with diffusers adjustable by dimmer switches to control the level of light on its display panels. The PRO at Chancery Lane where the exhibition room was refurbished at the end of 1990 uses dimmable, ultra-violet filtered, fluorescent tubes for background lighting and fibre-optic lighting for emphasis.

10 *The exhibition room at the Public Record Office, Chancery Lane.* Museum design, John Dangerfield Associates; specialist fibre optics Absolute Actions of London; photograph by Marianne Majerus.

Chapter 8
Conversion of existing buildings[1]

'The preferred option was, and would still be, a purpose-built repository, but the cost of a new building large enough to accommodate public, staff and records was quite beyond what the County Council was willing, or indeed able, in the present economic climate, to meet'.[2]

'If an old factory, or disused industrial warehouse were used there would be a risk of giving the impression that archives are a service of little importance, one for which any sort of old building is suitable' [Duchein p.30].

Having looked at a number of general principles governing archive buildings, we can now return to a consideration of the choice between a purpose-built record repository and the conversion of an existing building conceived for another purpose.

In practice the decision is influenced by political and financial considerations, by the priority and prestige accorded to archives in the local scheme of things, and by the competing claims upon capital resources including land.

Planning a purpose-built repository ought in principle to give archivist and architect more scope to make specifications (and achieve results) in line with BS 5454 for every aspect of the development. In particular, it may offer more opportunity to influence or control the choice of site and materials; the design, structure, layout and orientation; the internal environment, and the furnishings, equipment and lines of communication that make for a pleasant and efficient working environment.

As one writer puts it, purpose-building enables the architect to design the space to fit the operation, whereas conversion frequently has to mean fitting the operation into the available space [Haymond p.14].

Nevertheless, there can be advantages in the conversion of an existing building:

- it may be significantly cheaper

- it may be the only way to obtain a town-centre site

- it may be quicker than commissioning new work

- broadly speaking, the building's advantages and disadvantages will be apparent in advance, whereas in the case of new buildings they may be difficult to visualise from the drawing board

- it may provide the opportunity to recycle an otherwise redundant building, minimising the call upon new land or material resources [Haymond p.13], and if the building is itself both historic and dignified this may have its influence on the image of the archive service [Reimann].

Buildings give out signals to the community, to the staff and public who work there, and even to passers-by. One archivist commented that it was impossible to imagine, from the unprepossessing exterior of the building and the run-down nature of the district in which it had been located, what treasures could possibly be contained within its walls. More fortunate colleagues can boast of their uncovenanted blessings: panelled walls (Bradford) or art deco washrooms (Tyne and Wear). It *does* matter what sort of a building is taken on, and where.

A recent Environmental Action Guide from the Department of the Environment observed that:

Dilapidated under-maintained building stock and land are environmental eyesores. They help create a prevailing sense of urban environmental squalor. They also reflect false economy and, in the long run, wasteful asset management.

Drab buildings in otherwise abandoned areas may also encourage vandalism.

Each candidate must be judged on its own merits, and it may be necessary to reject a number of offers before an acceptable one finally emerges. This is never a painless decision, particularly if the need to move is urgent. But it is important to hold out against a patently unacceptable building: funding bodies make decisions of this scale in respect of their archives very infrequently, and mistakes cannot easily be rectified after occupancy.

The Commission has advised archivists to ask many questions:

- How big is the building? Is the area/volume sufficient for projected needs? If it is too big, what will be done with the unwanted space? Can it be heated/cooled economically and efficiently? If it is too small are there possibilities for lateral or vertical extension, now or in future?

- What was its former use? Did this require similar floor loadings, fire-proofing or security? If so has the building stood up well to the stress? If it was not designed with heavy loads in mind, will the foundations and floors bear the weights required? How important is it to preserve the building's original character, or indeed to campaign against that despite the insistence of planners, and what sort of image of the archive service will that building convey to the local community?

- How is the available space sub-divided? Will existing compartments appropriately meet the new requirements? In particular, will it be possible to site functions sensibly. If the building is not to be owned by the parent authority but only leased, will the landlord allow necessary alterations?

Are the floors of adjacent rooms at the same level?

- Are the premises free-standing, or built on to one or more properties, or just part of a larger building? In the two latter cases, who are the neighbours/co-tenants? Are any of their activities actually or potentially incompatible with the purposes of an archive building?

- Is there anything else about the structure of the building that might prove difficult or inconvenient? Consider, for example:

  excessive amounts of wood (fire hazard)

  flat roofs (see p.27)

  poorly insulated roofs (heat gain/loss, condensation)

  flimsy or fragile roofs (fracture, collapse, storm damage)

  skylights (leaks, intruders, heat gain/loss)

  flaking or crumbling internal walls (dust)

  asbestos used in walls, ceilings and lagging (health and safety)

  a super-abundance of windows (light, security)[3]

  basements (flooding, damp)

  fireplaces and chimneys (fire, environmental hazard)

  very high ceilings (waste of space, heat)

  very low ceilings (restricted racking, air circulation, services)

  columns or other structural supports (see p.27)

  heating systems and other services already in place (Study particularly the nature and location of inherited plant, water and sewerage services (especially if any of these run vertically or horizontally through or above the proposed storage areas), fuel tanks etc.)

★

There is no short cut to subjecting candidates to a thorough test. Some will emerge triumphant: fine, sturdy old buildings on town-centre sites offering ample space and convenient access, with floor loadings measured, as one observer put it, in 'elephants per square foot'. Others may seem just right as buildings but be in an impossible location, or perhaps vice-versa. Many will be suitable in most respects, while having a few unconquerable inconveniences, which will either have to be lived with, mitigated or compensated for by other provisions, or in the final resort cause the project to fail.

So in many instances it will be necessary to judge whether the compromises that have to be made with the ideal are prejudicial to the records. BS 5454 should remain the yardstick, but further guidance may be sought either from the Commission or from one of the other inspecting bodies.

In a number of European cities [Reimann], and indeed further afield also, as a matter of social policy archives have been deliberately housed in converted historic buildings, more as a means of maintaining a dignified cultural use for a redundant edifice which the local authority is statutorily or morally obliged to preserve than of finding a suitable home for the records. Michel Duchein has taken the view that occupation of a historic building in preference to a purpose-built repository is only justified if it is the only means of staying in the town centre [Duchein 1988, p.187].

Age, certainly, is not of itself a disadvantage. But not all old buildings are of a suitable calibre. Some will rule themselves out on structural grounds: lack of fire-resistance, awkward stairs, compartments or entrances, the difficulty or impossibility of adaptation to the needs of the record repository (for example installing lifts or air-conditioning, or meeting today's requirements of access for the disabled), or for a number of other practical reasons.

Buildings listed as of historic interest do not *ipso facto* make ideal repositories for historic records. Nor should the romantic notion be fostered that archives are somehow happier if stored in old buildings. Each case must be judged on its individual merits. Their adaptation, internal or external, can be seriously constrained if the character of the original building has to be preserved inviolate in order to comply with planning or historic building regulations. And yet, even within these constraints, some more than happy solutions have been found, given just the right combination of local circumstances.

In this country a great variety of buildings have been converted more or less successfully into record repositories. They include barracks, car showrooms, castles, churches, warehouses, factories and other industrial premises, hospitals, hotels, houses, a medieval guildhall, maltings, a military bunker, NAAFIs, a post office headquarters, prisons, a rectory and schools. Warehouses and schools, perhaps because they are among those most likely to be redundant in present circumstances, have been most commonly chosen for conversion. Churches are currently out of fashion, but ought not on that account to be overlooked.

Warehouses

Some warehouses converted in this period have proved extremely successful, others less so, one or two well-nigh disastrous. One thing to bear in mind is that warehoused goods in general are only in store for short periods, whereas the records are for permanent custody.

Warehouses come in many shapes and forms depending on the nature of the goods formerly stored there: single and multi-storey; built to last for ever, or purely to provide functional shelter as cheaply as possible; designed for commodities with high or low value; offering strict or only limited security. Their former use may give important clues to the standards to which the buildings must have been designed, for example in security, floor-loading and fire-resistance, which in turn may say

11 Converted
warehouse: Bristol
Record Office
(above).

12 Converted
warehouse: Cheshire
Record Office (right).

something of their likely suitability as archive buildings.

Age may prove an advantage. Solidly-built Victorian brick warehouses like the bonded warehouse converted by Bristol Record Office, the textile warehouse of Tyne and Wear, and the railway warehouse for the Museum of Science and Industry in Manchester are fortress-like, built to last. Their thick walls should contribute to environmental stability. Recently constructed warehouses, of the breeze-block and corrugated metal variety in particular (e.g. North Yorkshire, West Devon, Church of England Record Centre), tend to be altogether flimsier, and more transitory in concept: they need far more rigorous examination.

What they all have in common is ample storage space, generally open-plan or only sparingly partitioned. This may be a bane or a blessing depending on the particular scheme of development proposed. The storage accommodation in Tyne and Wear's building divides naturally into blocks, only some of which have as yet been occupied. This allows for modular expansion when necessary. In addition, the availability of a great area of cheap floor space has led the record office, despite the very strong floors available, to opt for cheaper static rather than mobile racking. Cheshire Record Office, a converted warehouse and furniture depository, is composed of convenient blocks around a central courtyard, enabling the storage area to be clearly separated from the other functions.

Most of the problems associated with warehouses have concerned the stability of their basic structure, and the means of heating, ventilating and otherwise protecting their great volumes of storage space.

Factories and industrial premises which have housed heavy machinery hold out similar promise on account of their substantial and proven floor-loading capacities and/or their large floor spaces. They include, for example, the Greater London Record Office (a former printing works), and the Greater Manchester County Record Office (a former textile factory).

Schools

Next to warehouses and industrial premises, schools make up the largest group of buildings converted for record storage in this period. The former Bedfordshire Record Office (1956) was one of the first to occupy a school. The most unusual case in this period is the Tudor grammar school at Shrewsbury converted to house the city library and its local studies department.[4] More commonly, buildings chosen have been of Victorian or later date. The separate classrooms afford a modest amount of ready-made compartmentation for offices, workshops and non-archival storage, and are especially well suited for educational services. Large windows admit plenty of natural light (indeed, sometimes too much) for search rooms or conservation workshops. Large school halls may be readily adaptable into strongrooms (Doncaster, Gloucestershire, Walsall) or search rooms (Ipswich, Lichfield). Playgrounds offer space for car-parking or for immediate or future expansion, and are fenced or railed off from the surrounding properties and streets, assisting perimeter security. Generally the location in relation to public transport is good. This in turn may reduce the need for the repository to be in the town centre.

Some schools are fine buildings in their own right, and where already owned by the same authority that will run the archive service it may make good sense to recycle them in the public service. Moreover, with falling school rolls and resulting closures, they may be available for the asking.

That is not to say that they are ideal in every case. Problems referred to the Commission have included:

- a tendency for the rooms, or in some cases buildings, to be strung out over a large horizontal axis, with many interconnecting doors and unnecessarily wide corridors, in some cases making for awkward lines of communication (This is by no means always the case, and indeed in some such buildings the use of the central hall as the new storage area actually improves lines of communication)

- flat roofs or multiple gables (see p.27)

- many external doors (security risk unless some are blocked)

- excessive height in some of the rooms (but there are cases where this has been put to good use, as at Walsall where it has allowed space to fit trunking for air conditioning and fire-extinction equipment, or Gloucestershire where the space was sufficient to accommodate a mezzanine floor)

- too many, or too large, windows, contributing to solar gain and heat loss respectively at different times (Walsall blocked up its south-facing windows but retained those on the north side)

- relatively shallow foundations unsuited to the installation of mobile racking

- the move being seized on by the authority as the lowest-cost option, involving little capital outlay because it owned the building already, in some cases not even running to a lick of paint (It may be difficult for the archivist to sustain the argument that a record repository should be a bright and cheerful place in which to work if this was not the case in the school which preceded it).

The existence of large playgrounds or other surrounding land has enabled Leicestershire, Lichfield and Suffolk Record Offices to combine the conversion of an existing school for search room and offices with a new purpose-built storage block for the records, and Gloucestershire to put purpose-built extensions on to its converted school.

Churches

In earlier centuries, churches were commonly used as places of safety for the storage of records. In our own day, with the growth of alternative secular provision their role in this respect has been sharply reduced, and in England under the provisions of successive Parochial Registers and Records Measures even the parishes' own historic records have now mainly been moved to a safer, more controlled environment in the diocesan record office.

But at the same time there has been a steady flow of redundant churches on to the property market, and a few have been converted into record repositories. Within the dates covered by this volume only one church has been converted in this way, to house the library of the London Hospital, with the archives in the crypt, but there have been major up-gradings or refurbishments of churches already converted before 1977, including St Helen's Worcester, and the Hampshire (to 1993) and Cambridgeshire (Huntingdon) Record Offices. Another former church, in Charlotte Square, Edinburgh (converted 1969/70) continues in use as the West Register House of the Scottish Record Office.

There are some advantages: the sheer volume of potential storage space, inner city sites, the sympathetic use of a historic building, an aesthetic and (at least to some) inspiring working environment for staff and public, perhaps even with stained glass windows in the search room. It would be unwise to dismiss such buildings out of hand.

But there are undeniable problems, the chief of which concern the form and condition of the fabric. It may be one of the terms of occupancy that the shell of the building be left unaltered and the walls of the storage areas constructed within, but clear of the outer walls of the original building, and this may be no cheap option. If the development extends upwards through several levels in order to maximise the use of the vertical space, arches, pillars and other original architectural features may get in the way. The same problem may arise in the horizontal plane, with pillars, side chapels and apses restricting and dictating the positioning of shelving, furniture and partitions. Control of temperature and relative humidity may prove difficult or at least expensive, especially if original large windows are preserved.

And how sound is the fabric? Almost anyone with experience on a parochial church council will have encountered the costs and liabilities of church fabric: typically, leaking roofs, damp walls (resulting, for example, from gutters blocked by falling leaves), crumbling or flaking masonry, eroded stone or brickwork.

13 Converted church: Hampshire Record Office (to 1993).

Will buckets be needed to catch the drips? Will pinnacles fall down in a gale and damage the roof? Will the roof need replacing? These have all happened in converted churches in this period. Great height, multiple roofs with many angles and much flashing, extraneous ornamentation: all can make for difficulties with regard to archive storage, and should be weighed very carefully before a decision is taken to convert a church building for long-term archive storage.

★

The archivist whose only practical option is to look for a building to convert should bear in mind first that 'conversion' is the operative word: some degree of real adaptation will be necessary because buildings do not come ready-made for archive storage; and secondly that even in a conversion the aim should be to match as nearly as possible what could be achieved in a purpose-building [Bell 1979, p. 83]. Conversely, those designing a purpose-building should take time to identify and avoid the worst inconveniences associated with adaptations. There is no excuse nowadays for creating from scratch an archive building that wilfully falls short of the standard or has built-in inconveniences (such as narrow corridors with tight turns, or spiral staircases). The most important consideration is whether it will provide a secure and healthy environment for the records it is to house.

1.   Among works cited in the Bibliography, those by Duchein and Nicol are particularly relevant, as well as the papers under the citation *Archive buildings and the conservation of archival material* pp.218–25, 262–4.

2.   Ian Dunn, writing in Norton, p.23.

3.   There is some evidence that boarded-up windows tempt vandals, see Nicol in Norton, p.20.

4.   See the article on Shrewsbury Castlegates Library in Harrison 1987, pp.182–4 and Field, R and Crow, T, 'Castle Gates Library . . ., Telford Town Centre Library and Stirchley Library' in Dewe 1989.

Appendix to Chapter 8

A note on shared premises

In some of the cases studied for this survey (and many others not mentioned) the archive service occupies only part of a larger building. This is the norm in the case of local authority and university libraries and national and local museums, irrespective of whether the building is purpose-built or a conversion. It also applies where record offices are located in county halls as at Berkshire or West Glamorgan.

Sharing can be beneficial to both staff and public when it unites under one roof kindred reference and cultural services. The North Devon Record Office at Barnstaple shares a building with the library, the North Devon Athenaeum, the Tourist Information Office and the Citizens' Advice Bureau. The Colchester branch of the Essex Record Office is housed alongside the registrar of births, marriages and deaths, the consumer protection office and the magistrates' clerks. Sharing

may also be beneficial to under-resourced services if there can be some exchange between, for example, library and archives staff at peak hours or during staff leave.

The security, storage and environmental requirements specific to the archives must however be separately planned and monitored. Shared accommodation may prove problematic if it leaves outside the archivist's responsibility the control of the other parts of the building and the activities carried on there, some of which might represent potential hazards to the archives. This is particularly true if those activities are carried on outside the opening hours of the repository. If space in the overall development is very tight, there can also be a danger of the archive service (which as already stated needs ample space for expansion) being boxed in, as at Barnstaple and Croydon, or of any overflow storage being scattered within the building as at the British Library of Political and Economic Science.

Chapter 9
Functions: some practical hints

The concept of the segregation of functions into blocks for planning purposes was touched on in chapter 1, mainly in relation to security and fire prevention. Another practical consideration is noise. Much of the work undertaken in an archive building requires concentration. This can be assisted not only by strategically separating incompatible activities, but also by planning lines of communication, and providing appropriately thick walls, and floor, ceiling and wall coverings that will absorb sound. Ideally, each function or area should be accessible without passing through another. Inter-connected rooms with no corridors to by-pass them promote excessive traffic.

Noise inside the building can originate from: plant and machinery; lift doors and motors; vibrations carried along ducting, piping and wall surfaces; speech and laughter from enquiry desks, offices, lecture theatres, classrooms, staff rooms, kitchens and common rooms; typewriters and tape-recorders; radios and televisions used for educational purposes or (if allowed) in workshops; the slamming of doors and flushing of lavatories. Noise can also be generated from adjacent properties, or wholly from outside by traffic, aircraft, passers-by, building work or industrial activity, all of which should be taken into account when choosing the site.

Poor examples met in the course of this study include an education room accessible only by way of the public search room; a proposed seminar room separated from the searchroom on one side and staff offices on the other only by a thin partition wall; WCs with *fortissimo* plumbing just off the search room; and single-glazed public search rooms fronting on to busy main roads.

★

It is important not to become so obsessed with the importance of functional segregation as to miss the equally important inter-relationships. The links can be represented diagrammatically, as in figure 5. It should be noted, however, that this is not a blue-print for the physical lay-out of the building, but only an indication of the relationships between functions. It is not based on any one building, and should not be used as a model without taking account of local conditions and preferences. Larger repositories devising such charts sometimes vary the thickness of the flow-lines to represent the relative volumes of traffic.

Translating this into a ground-plan, especially in a converted building, is the main challenge. Generally, the more spread out the functions laterally or vertically, the more difficult the building is to manage economically and securely. And lines of communication, both horizontal and vertical, need special attention. What routes will (a) the records and (b) the people follow within the building? What mechanical assistance will be necessary (lifts, hoists, trolleys etc), and at what points? What obstacles (doors, stairs, corners etc) will be encountered in transit, and with what consequences for the building's security and environmental specifications and fire precautions?

Once again, some poor examples might be mentioned: storage areas above or below the level of the search room but with no lift or book hoist to connect them; awkward right-angle bends in corridors adding difficulty to the movement of outsize documents; storage areas situated a route march away from the search room with several locked doors in between; lifts opening directly on to the storage areas or the search room. It is always

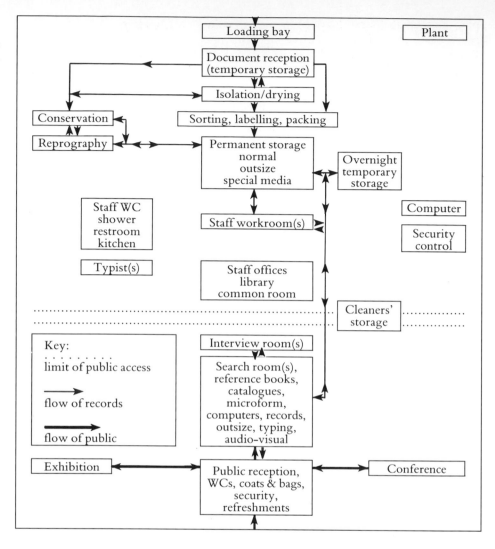

Figure 5
Relationship between
functions in an archive
building.

Loading bay   Plant

Document reception
(temporary storage)

Isolation/drying

Conservation

Sorting, labelling, packing

Reprography

Permanent storage
normal
outsize
special media

Overnight
temporary
storage

Staff WC
shower
restroom
kitchen

Staff workroom(s)

Computer

Security
control

Typist(s)

Staff offices
library
common room

Cleaners'
storage

Key:
. . . .
limit of public access

⟶
flow of records

━━━▶
flow of public

Interview room(s)

Search room(s),
reference books,
catalogues,
microform,
computers, records,
outsize, typing,
audio-visual

Exhibition

Public reception,
WCs, coats & bags,
security,
refreshments

Conference

---

useful to have an experienced independent eye cast over the plans before building commences!

★

With these issues in mind we can now follow the various functions through the diagram, noting some of the practical points which have arisen in archive buildings of this period.[1]

★

Delivery bay

A covered delivery bay, foregone as an economy measure in a few instances, protects records from the elements. It needs to be covered by the intruder alarm system, especially if out of sight at the rear of the building, and for added security should be openable only from the inside. Additional surveillance by closed-circuit TV, entry phones and security lighting is sometimes provided. Where canopies or drive-in bays are used, their ceiling and any projections such as gutters have to allow for the highest vehicle expected and, if the land slopes, for the tilt of the vehicle also. Vehicles and buildings alike have had unfortunate scrapes where this was overlooked. Loading platforms of fixed heights have also caused logistical problems, and a mechanical platform/hoist (West Sussex), a metal roller conveyor belt (Glasgow University Business Records Centre) or a fork-lift truck (Greater Manchester) may be desirable alternative or additional equipment.

The importance of getting across to all concerned at the outset of the project the nature and special requirements of an archive building is illustrated by one or two cases in which, alas, property services departments thinking they were doing the right thing by the records have sought as their prospective archive building a warehouse equipped with large doors to enable vehicles to drive right inside! One repository as a result still bears indoor signs with the legend 'Maximum Speed 5 mph', although vehicles have now been banished and a new drive-in delivery bay has been created, separated from the repository by an internal wall and a door. Vehicles pose a risk of fire, dirt, damp, environmental pollution and noise, and the opening of a large section of the outer defences, however temporarily, is a threat both to security and to the stability of the internal environment (which is likely to have been controlled only at considerable cost).

Reception room(s)

Adjacent to the delivery bay there is usually a reception room/area where the records may be examined, and any needing treatment for mould or insect infestation may be identified and isolated. Storage space unimpeded by columns, heaters etc is a welcome asset here. Fittings such as shelves or pigeon-holes and tables vary with local preference. Hampshire's new building includes in addition a *cleaning room* for particularly dirty documents. In Lincolnshire the sorting benches in the reception area, which is divided into five work-stations, are fitted with vacuum suction tubes for initial cleaning.

Where modern records management is offered, that may require its own reception room.

Drying

Fumigation of contaminated records is now discouraged,[2] and the smell of thymol which used to enable the *cognoscenti* to make their way through county hall or university corridors to the record office is therefore regarded with concern. Accordingly fumigation rooms, which used to be thought essential, have been abandoned or converted to other uses, mainly to isolate records infested with mould and allow them to acclimatise in a controlled environment. A number of repositories are adding freezers to their reception equipment, to deal at least temporarily with any in-coming material saturated by flood or fire-fighting water, or as part of their own disaster recovery plan.

Sorting room(s)

Over and above the space allocated for initial reception, it is usual to provide a separate room or rooms for sorting because the work

14   The reception area at Lincolnshire Archives.

can be dirty, requires ample space, and is not conveniently performed in a general office.

Storage room(s)

A good deal has already been said in earlier chapters about structural, security and environmental aspects of the storage areas. This section addresses some of the practical problems that have arisen.

(a) Newer media

Special provision is increasingly being made for the newer media. But where attempts have been made to house them in an environment controlled separately from that in the rest of the repository, numerous difficulties have been encountered in sufficiently reducing the relative humidity in a cool room. With this in mind, Hampshire has decided, at least in the first instance, not to introduce a separate environment for the Wessex Film and Sound Archive, but to keep it in what should prove naturally the coolest part of the building, with the air-handling plant near to hand should remedial action prove necessary. Some repositories have standing arrangements instead to transfer archives in these media to regional film and sound archives. What can be achieved in specialist centres with the backing of necessarily large investment is well illustrated by the case of the National Film Archive which has introduced special dehumidification equipment and has effectively established separate environments for the various media in its care.

(b) Large documents

Large documents including maps and plans are sometimes also stored in separate rooms. This is the norm in the large, national repositories, but occurs locally also. Cornwall Record Office, for example, has devoted one strong room entirely to map storage, employing backward-sloping racking originally designed for shop use. Fittings elsewhere vary, from purpose-built wooden shelving suspended from the walls (West Sussex) to Italian supermarket shelving (Devon).

(c) Special storage

Some repositories set aside a room with a greater degree of security for the storage of more valuable or confidential items.

(d) Temporary storage

It is useful, as in Northamptonshire, to designate specific space adjacent to the search room for holding documents on call until they are required. With appropriate environmental controls this may assist them to acclimatise between the differing environments of the strongroom and the search room.

(e) Wooden racking

Opinion is divided on the merits of using wooden racking. The basic requirement of BS 5454 [s.9.1.2] is that the material should be 'durable and non-combustible'. It used to be thought quite straightforward that metal was always preferable, and wood to be avoided because it was flammable and might give out acids which would harm the archival materials or react with metals such as lead in papal bulls

15　Map storage:
Cornwall Record
Office (left).

16　Map storage:
West Sussex Record
Office (right).

or window lights and metallic silver in photographs. On the other hand wood of a suitable quality and thickness and appropriately treated is both sturdy and durable. If treated with flame-retardant, it will tend in the event of fire to smoulder for a considerable time before igniting. It can also be sealed (though not with an inflammable oil) to prevent acids leaching out, and that risk may be further lessened by storing the archives in acid-free boxes. A case was reported to the Society of Archivists Conference in 1991 from a library which had a mixture of wooden and metal racking and was unfortunate enough to suffer a fire. The metal racking buckled in the heat and collapsed, while the wooden racking although charred remained intact. Many archive buildings do in fact rely on wooden or wood-product shelving. The only safe advice is to review the choice in the light of the overall strategy on fire and environmental control.

(f) Mobile racking

Where floor-loadings have permitted, and funds run to it, most new repositories have

17　Mobile racking
at Suffolk Record
Office, Ipswich.
Stelstor.

employed mobile racking to maximise the use of storage space. At Hereford and Worcester (HQ) it was calculated that mobile racking although twice as expensive as static would enable a 30% saving in size and 20% in cost of building. Where there is no shortage of space for lateral expansion, and/or where space is not particularly expensive, as in Tyne and Wear Record Office, this may be an expensive option.

(g) Space for plant

Above the racking, whether static or mobile, sufficient space must be allowed to facilitate ventilation and/or allow for the installation of any necessary trunking and services. Calculating the space required, and the knock-on effects on shelving capacity, has sometimes proved difficult, for example when Cornwall Record Office was extended and air-conditioning introduced in 1987–88. Dorset and Gloucestershire lost some of their expected storage capacity on the same grounds.

(h) Emergency communications

The wisdom of installing telephones in the storage area was demonstrated in the early days of one new repository when the air-circulation system malfunctioned and began extracting air. The resulting pressure prevented the archivist opening the strongroom door from inside, and assistance had to be called on the emergency telephone. Another problem, specific to a windowless strongroom, is total darkness in the event of a power failure. To overcome this, rechargeable torches are commonly provided. At Hereford and Worcester a fluorescent strip has been attached to the end of each system of racking to mark the way to the exit.

Staff room(s) for production and delivery of documents

Larger repositories, such as the PRO and the National Library of Wales, require a room or rooms adjacent to the storage area(s) to accommodate the staff who control the pro-

duction and delivery of documents. In Lincolnshire, where requisitioning is being computerised, a separate dust-proof and sound-proof room has been provided on each floor to house a computer printer and also the staff who service the requests.

★

Conservation workshop

The United Kingdom's archive repositories are justifiably renowned for their conservation services, and are the envy of many in the museum and library world who have no in-house facilities.

The most important considerations for a conservation workshop are that it should be safe and comfortable to work in, conforming with the Control of Substances Hazardous to Health regulations, and ergonomically efficient, assisting the flow of work from one piece of equipment to the next in logical sequence. Presses and other heavy equipment require substantial floor-loadings. The check-list of essential services includes plenty of power-points; sink(s) and running water with associated drainage services all preferably sited on outside walls and fitted with external overflows to prevent any mishap in the workshop; and a safe system for the extraction of fumes. Ample storage space is required for materials, and lockable storage for chemicals. Generous space is desirable, to cater for the full complement of staff and equipment projected over the lifetime of the building, but also to allow for the preparation and assembly of exhibitions, the repair of unusually large documents, and circulation space for training and demonstrations. Some conservators – as in Dorset and Lincolnshire Record Offices (purpose-built) and Greater London Record Office (conversion) – have designed their own workshops. Several model layouts have been published [Roper 1989, p.68; Woods p.132], and a number of permutations are possible. But success depends in part on the size, shape and orientation of the premises.

Dorset's spacious and well equipped conservation workshop (a long rectangle of 1,100 sq ft) may be taken as a model. It is air-conditioned, at a relative humidity of 58% to match that in the storage areas, with a constant temperature of 18–19°C. Its windows are filtered against ultra-violet light and coated to eliminate solar gain. There is ample circulating and man-oeuvring space throughout the working area. Wet and dry processes are housed at opposite ends of the room and a large work bench occupies the centre, with materials stored below. Considerable attention has been paid to the dimensions of workbenches and storage equipment. A tilting light-box and a back-lit 8 mm perspex wall board for repairing maps and large documents have been purpose-designed. The floor surface is non-slip and resistant to water and most chemical spillage, and in all aspects of design, health and safety has been taken into account [Woods]. Among alternative practices noted, the wet area in the workshop at the PRO of Northern Ireland (1979/80) is housed in the ante-room separated from the main workshop by a glazed partition. Here (as elsewhere) under-floor trunking was laid for the electricity supply to work benches and other equipment.[3]

Reprographics

The Public Record Office has easily the largest archival reprographics unit in the country, with machinery and equipment on a scale not encountered elsewhere. Among local authority repositories, Lincolnshire has the most advanced reprographics facilities, with a photography studio and a suite of six rooms for processing microfilm, fiche and black and white and colour photographs. This required special air-handling plant to ensure thorough ventilation in the windowless rooms. North Yorkshire, which microfilms all its holdings as a matter of course, has a correspondingly large microfilm unit. Some contract out the service entirely. Facilities to be considered for any check-list include *camera room(s)*, *dark room(s)*, where a water supply will be required, *work and rest space for the staff*, and sufficient *storage* space for chemicals and materials.[4]

Other storage and service space

Further storage space, in separate rooms or cupboards, is needed for boxes and packing materials, stationery stores, and cleaning

18 *Conservation workshop at Lincolnshire Archives.*

materials respectively. This, unfortunately, is another amenity commonly sacrificed when budgets run thin. Cleaners may need other resources: West Sussex Record Office is in advance of the field in having a separate room with a plumbed-in washer-drier.

Computer rooms

In a few instances only, rooms have been specially designed to house the central computer and related equipment. The PRO has recently fitted out a new computer room at Kew, air-conditioned and provided with a raised floor to conceal the cables.

Offices for professional and ancillary staff

Staff offices are the regular working environment and should take into account the individual's need for designated territory, the right balance between isolation when required (for example for interviews and confidential discussions) and awareness of the surrounding environment both inside and outside the building. Managers generally require their own reasonably sound-proof rooms, and not a shared room or part of an open-plan office. At less senior levels, some sharing of offices among two to four staff remains common and in some cases is indeed preferred.

Staff library

Larger repositories with considerable holdings of reference books for staff use, as in the national repositories or, for example, at West Sussex, or those housing another organisation such as a records society as at Northamptonshire, have sometimes designated special rooms as libraries.

Other staff facilities

British, unlike many French, archive buildings do not normally include a residential flat for the archivist in charge. Dumfries Archive Centre, occupying what was once a house, began life with a nicely equipped bathroom but had to replace it with fitted storage cupboards.[5] There is however an encouraging trend towards provision of one or more staff *showers* for decontamination after work on dirty documents (Calderdale, Dorset, Notts, W Sussex), and *rest rooms* equipped at the minimum with a bed and if possible a wash basin, and located as near as possible to a WC (Dorset, Suffolk, W Sussex).

In all but the smallest repositories, the staff are normally provided with WC and washroom facilities separate from those used by the public. Where, exceptionally, these have to be located in common parts of a shared building, they can be kept private by means of a combination lock, as at Merseyside Record Office. It is also appropriate to provide a *kitchen* or *common-room*, combined or separate, for staff breaks.

Plant

Special precautions have widely been taken in plant areas against fire and flood: not only heat- and water-detectors and alarms (since these areas may be left unattended for long periods), but also structural precautions to prevent trouble spreading to any other part of the building in the event of a malfunction. It is preferable not to locate plant below, beside or above the storage areas, but separated from them at least by a corridor and vented through an outside wall. Where water tanks and boilers have to be sited adjacent to, and on a level with, the storage areas, additional precautions have sometimes been necessary, including the installation of flood sills to strongroom doors. Access may be required to plant rooms outside normal office hours, so it is helpful to have a separate means of entry from the exterior, which does not give access to other parts of the building.

The PRO at Kew, which requires huge plant, has buried most of it in the sub basement, but with detached exhaust vents in a separate structure. At Dorset, where the space for plant was under-estimated in the early plans, there was eventually no alternative to housing it in the roof space, which has accordingly been fitted with fire and flood alarms and tanked and externally drained. At West Sussex the plant room occupies much of one side of the building, separated from the strong rooms by a corridor.

Several repositories have heating provided from a detached boiler unit (Hampshire 1993, Lancashire, Worcester). Within the repository, heating and water and electrical services including computer cabling are increasingly being carried in the wall space to minimise risks to the records. Wherever possible, in order to conserve energy, plant supplying hot water should be located close to the relevant service points. Individual water heaters might be considered as an alternative in washrooms and kitchens.

In converted buildings inherited services require special vigilance. In a recent upgrading of the accommodation at the Suffolk Record Office at Lowestoft it was necessary to fit an internal gutter below existing water pipes which traverse the ceiling of the storage area, with a flood alarm for added security, whilst heating pipes have been insulated and covered in aluminium cladding to prevent heat gain in the repository.

In some cases, including the PRO and Suffolk Record Office (Ipswich) it has been necessary to install dedicated electricity sub-stations to serve the repository and guarantee a steady power supply.

PUBLIC AREAS

Reception

In the best modern designs the public enter the building through a unique and well signed entrance. Many of the buildings featured in this book have a staffed reception area where readers sign in, apply for admission tickets where necessary, and ask preliminary questions. It is normal to include, off or adjacent to this area, the *public WCs* and *cloakrooms or*

lockers for coats and bags, and any *common-room* or *canteen* for the public. The PRO restaurant at Kew may be unique in advertising a 'full English breakfast', but it is becoming the norm now for archive buildings to include facilities where readers may eat their own food, make cups of tea or coffee or at least buy drinks from a vending machine. For some readers research time is hard-earned and their breaks need to be as short as possible. Unless good and plentiful refreshment facilities are available close by, some such provision should now be considered standard.

Among the other services associated with the reception area, space is sometimes provided, as in Essex and Suffolk Record Offices, and the Caernarfon Area Record Office, for the *display and sale of publications*, or, as in Kent, for a more general sales-point.

Facilities for the *disabled* are gradually being improved. This affects planning of doors, steps/ramps, lifts and WCs in particular. In converted buildings access for the disabled is not always readily achievable, and there are still too many older buildings, even among those which have been converted in this period for archival use, with stairs but no lift. The addition of a new storage block gave Lancashire Record Office the opportunity to cater for disabled visitors by means of a lift to the search room, which is on the first floor and had previously been approachable only by steps. At Hereford and Worcester (HQ) access is by means of a gentle, though unfortunately rather long ramp. Attention to fixtures and fittings has been a special feature at Northamptonshire Record Office where, for example, a public telephone has been installed at wheelchair height.

Exhibition area[6]

Exhibitions are always popular with visitors and attract a wider public. Increasingly the practice is to site an exhibition area in or near reception in order to make it as accessible as possible to the general public without increasing disturbance elsewhere in the building.

BS 5454 deals with exhibitions in some detail [s.12]. It emphasises that wherever original records as distinct from reproductions are displayed, security, environmental and lighting controls should match those in the permanent storage areas. The area may require special security alarms and adequate means of invigilation perhaps with the use of CCTV if the area is not permanently staffed, ultra-violet screens and/or blinds for the windows (if any), unimpeded wall space and room for free-standing screens or display cases. The exhibition room at Dorset, off the public entrance, is carpeted and the windows are fitted with screens and blinds. Electrical trunking within the skirting board allows some flexibility in the siting of power points. Renewable display panels of painted blockboard are fixed six inches proud of the walls by wooden supports, and on the main walls a picture rail allows for hanging.

Search room(s)

A recent survey conducted by Chester City Record Office[7] concluded that 'serious' researchers liked the search room to be quiet and needed plenty of space. They also disliked other researchers sitting too close! For most visitors this is the main port of call. Improved standards of decor, lighting, furniture and carpeting, are everywhere contributing to a more comfortable working environment. Decorations and furnishings in light tones, not so strikingly bright as to be a distraction [Thompson 1963, p.6] (but not gloomy either), can provide a calm and pleasant setting. Carpets, curtains and noise-absorbing ceiling materials also help to minimise disturbance. Where computers are likely to be used for research, requisitioning, or access to on-line data, adequate provision needs to be made not only for the cabling and power supplies, but also for the space occupied by the equipment.

The PRO at Kew was among the first to create a separate *reference room* for consultation of catalogues, indexes and other finding aids as well as personal enquiries about the records, in order to concentrate this potentially noisy activity in one place, at one stage removed from the search room. Smaller record offices may have no need for this degree of segregation, but it is gaining favour, sometimes with a common staff service point covering reference and search areas (Dorset, Greater London RO, Nottinghamshire). Reference areas do require some invigilation since finding aids, and particularly printed reference works, both of which may be irreplaceable, are prone to wander or be removed without authority. Where *local studies libraries* are an integral part of the service, magnetic or radio-frequency book alarm systems have sometimes been installed at the exit (N. Devon, Hereford & Worcester, Suffolk).

An *interview room* is occasionally provided, in which readers on their first visit or with particularly detailed research problems may meet a member of the professional staff. Cubicles whose walls do not extend to the ceiling have been tried in some places but found unsatisfactory.

Depending on the scale of the operation, the nature of the holdings, and again on local practice, distinct areas if not distinct rooms can be provided for the respective consultation of *microfilm*, *traditional media* (records on paper and parchment), and *out-size documents* especially maps. This however can present staffing, managerial and logistical problems, with readers perhaps coming and going across each others' paths and requiring assistance and/or invigilation in several separate areas simultaneously. Microfilm holdings are growing fairly generally, and this shift in the pattern of use needs to be taken into account when apportioning space.

Projecting the growth of reader visits over the whole life of the building is notoriously difficult. In the case of the PRO at Kew early projections proved far too generous, although the space quickly proved useful for other purposes. In some other cases, as at Berkshire and Cornwall Record Offices, insufficient space was allowed and the new facilities quickly became crowded.

Where *audio-visual records* are held, appropriate listening/viewing facilities should also be provided although in practice this has not always been done. Similarly where readers are permitted to use typewriters, computers or tape-recorders special provision should be made, including the necessary cabling and sound-proof cubicles if required, as at West Sussex. Booths which were not sound-proofed at Berkshire have now been turned over to other uses. The new Hampshire Record Office is the first general purpose record office in this country to be equipped with a cinema, albeit for wider use by the local authority.

Public meeting rooms

Policies and programmes for out-reach and public relations vary from one authority to another. Pressure is mounting, especially owing to the growing educational demand for access to original sources for study, for seminar, lecture and/or class-room facilities. Some record offices situated in converted former schools as at Ipswich and Walsall, lend themselves naturally to this. In other cases it requires more planning. For example, access to any such rooms should be either from the main reception area (West Sussex, Dorset, Caernarfon) or by means of a separate outer door (Cheshire). If the room is to be used outside normal opening hours a self-contained unit, with its own access and WCs, is preferable.

Since such rooms may not be in continuous use, and conversely may need to be open at hours when the rest of the office is closed, a number of record offices have planned for the space to be used as flexibly as possible. Dorset's education room, seating up to 100, has a door into the adjacent exhibition area. North-amptonshire and Caernarfon have movable partitions to allow the room to be extended into the reception area for other functions.

Meeting rooms intended for multiple purposes can usefully incorporate stacking space for chairs and tables, and lockable *storage space* for audio-visual and other equipment.

Where the staff includes, for example, an education officer, it will also be necessary to provide, near to the meeting room, a separate *office* for this purpose.

Expansion space

Not included on the flow diagram, but very definitely to be taken into account when planning, is the question of expansion space for the future, for all functions and services where an increased demand for space is to be expected.

1. Local practices vary widely as to the allocation of space between functions, and no attempt is made here to recommend standard or minimum dimensions. Some, such as minimum ceiling height, shelf height and width, and the width of doors and gangways, are the subject of BS 5454 recommendations. Useful guidance on individual rooms is given by Duchein and by Bell and Faye, but these and other authorities differ in detail.

2. See M Aleppo, 'Fumigation?', in *Archives*, 82 (October 1989), pp.74–7.

3. For more detailed guidance see Roper 1989.

4. For more detailed guidance see Keene & Roper.

5. M Stewart, 'Archives and local history in the south west', in *Scottish Local History*, 21, p.8.

6. On the environment in display cases see especially Thomson, *The Museum Environment* and also more detailed articles by him in *Studies in Conservation*, 9 (1964) pp.153–69 and 22 (1977), pp.85–105.

7. Business Plan 1991, p.28.

Appendix to Chapter 9

The brief for a new building

Depending on the speed with which a project must be seen through, and the working preferences of individual architects, it can be necessary to proceed through several separate stages of briefing, beginning with no more than an outline and working towards a definitive document or documents which will guide the architect, engineers, surveyors and contractors through every phase. It is advisable for archivist and architect to have at least a preliminary discussion of requirements before anything is committed to writing.

The most effective brief is one which combines clear direction with succinctness and is focused on the needs of the particular authority and service without lengthy diversions into the nature of archives, security, or other key concepts. The French *Manuel d'archivistique* [France, p.572] observes that with a good brief the architect cannot help produce a good building, whilst the archivist who draws up a deficient brief deserves all that is coming. Headings towards a brief are given at the end of this appendix.

One architect who had just designed a record office commented that there was nothing specially complex in his task once the building's functions and their relationships had been explained to him. By contrast, a county archivist who had just been complimented on the essential simplicity of the plan for a new building retorted that 'to conform to BS 5454 is anything but simple!'

It has been said that the main challenge to the architect lies in giving substance, form and style without confusing the building's proper priorities [Buchmann 1986 (2), p.211], and that 'form follows function' [Gondos 1964, p.477–8]. From time to time debate has been joined over the outward and visible manifestations of archive buildings. At the level of the national repository, dignity and a sense of the historic have been called for [Schellenberg p.88]. Sometimes, as in the foyer of the Bundesarchiv, Koblenz, the opportunity has been taken to commission works of art to humanise the building and assert its wider links with the culture of the community. British archive buildings have tended to be much more austere, although the design for the PRO at Kew was submitted for the approval of the Royal Fine Art Commission, and even in buildings of smaller scale such as the new county record offices considerable attention has often been paid to external detail, and a number of design awards have been won, for example for the excellence of the brickwork (Southampton university) or for skilful restoration of a historic building (Suffolk: Ipswich).

A few of the new buildings considered in this study, including both conversions and new buildings, evince little concern for the community, appearing to make a virtue of stark blank walls which to the uninitiated might more closely resemble the shell of a prison or nuclear reactor than a record repository. More commonly this danger has been foreseen and the external features softened in sympathy with their surroundings.

The architect's drawings, like the briefs from which they take their inspiration as to layout, orientation and general shape, are refinable documents. The first drafts in particular are for critical study, not uncritical admiration. Either at this stage or once they have been revised to take account of the archivist's initial comments, they are often referred for comment to the Commission and/or the other inspecting bodies. It is rare in the Commission's experience to find whole functions omitted in error or completely unviable layouts, but this consultative stage provides an opportunity to raise pertinent points with the architect and consider alternative layouts, for example to promote greater security or make the building more easily manageable.

Whilst it is the job of the architect to give expression and character to the building, this must not be at the expense of its functionality, and from time to time the archivist has to stand firm against misunderstandings of the essential requirements, or against 'the more imaginative vision' of the architect [Ian Dunn in Norton]. In West Sussex a gallery overlooking the search room, carrying the main thoroughfare between staff offices, had been left open in the architect's plans but was glazed in on the archivist's insistence in order to reduce noise and disturbance. In Northamptonshire the archivist pressed for return walls throughout the offices, strong enough to carry book shelves.

Headings towards a brief for an archive building

Overall considerations

The current state of play including:

- agreements and understandings already reached, budgetary commitments etc
- reasons why the new building is needed
- budgetary, timing and other constraints
- possible alternative strategies

The records held/to be held:

- their nature
- their use (by whom, for what purposes)

The objectives of the governing authority with regard to archives, including any published standards which it may wish to see adopted in the project: e.g.

- BS 5454
- Standard for record repositories

Any aspects of those Standards which it may wish to emphasise:

- the priority to be given to the secure custody of the records
- their protection against fire and flood, damp and heat, atmospheric and environmental pollution, dust, insects and vermin, unauthorised access and all other hazards
- stability of the internal environment

The authority's commitment to, or the building's need to comply with, other national or local policy directives, on matters such as:

- energy consumption
- environmental and ecological issues
- value for money, including the long term (e.g. ease of maintenance, management, communication)
- access for the disabled
- health and safety

The broad groups of functions to be housed in the building, and the desirability of separating archive storage from other functions

The main considerations affecting choice of site, structure and materials

Overall ambience, style and impact on the community

Any specific problems of the existing service which it is hoped will be overcome in the new building

Overall statistics of present and projected use, such as: [Bell 1979, p.84]

- quantity of records held now/rate of accrual in recent years
- number of records produced for inspection in a given time span (e.g. a year)
- number of public visits e.g. per day, per week, and their typical duration; recent overall trends; maximum to be provided for
- number of staff employed/to be employed

- need for car parking space, and impact of road access on local traffic

- expected duration of occupancy of new building/provision for expansion

- total floor space required (broken down by function below)

Any predictable changes in the nature or media of holdings or pattern of their accrual or use during the lifespan of the building

Individual functions and their relationship

For each function identified in the checklist:
Space
  area/volume required, special dimensional requirements
Nature of the activities
Special statutory or other requirements
  e.g. Health & Safety
Structural requirements
  floor-loading; orientation; provision/absence of windows

General ambience
  colour scheme; comfort; noise levels/acoustics
Security and fire precautions
Environmental controls
  temperature
  relative humidity
  ventilation
  lighting
Communications
  links to other functions
  telecommunications
  computer
Services
  power supply; number and location of points; isolation
  water supply; location of services and drainage
  sanitation; location and route of services
Furniture, equipment and machinery

Bibliography

For BS 5454 see under British Standards Institution. *JSA* indicates *Journal of the Society of Archivists*. Some further published articles about individual repositories are cited in the notes to the case studies and in the Appendix to Part 2.

Allsopp, B. *The modern theory of architecture* (1984).

Anderson, H. and McIntyre, JE. *Planning manual for disaster control in Scottish libraries and record offices* (National Library of Scotland, 1985).

[Anon.] 'Air conditioning for the preservation of Parliamentary archives', in *Heating and ventilation engineer*, Feb. 1962, pp.428–30.

[Anon.] 'Problems at the PRO', in *Architects' Journal*, 179 no 13 (1984), p.33.

Archive buildings and the conservation of archival material [proceedings of an expert meeting held in Vienna, 1985], in *Mitteilungen des Österreichischen Staatsarchivs*, 39 (1986), pp.197–289.

[Archivum]. *Modern buildings of national archives*: Archivum XXXI (1986).

Association of County Archivists. *Yesterday's future: a national policy for our archive heritage* (1983).

Ballantyne, D. 'Planning new facilities – building from experience', in *The Archivist* [Canada], 19 no 2 (1992), pp.18–19.

Belda, LS. 'Construction of archive buildings in the last ten years', in *Unesco Bulletin for Libraries*, XXVIII (1964), pp.20–6.

Bell, L. 'Archival accommodation in the United Kingdom', in *JSA*, 6 (1980), pp.345–64.

Bell, L. 'The archivist and his accommodation', in *Archivaria*, VIII (1979), pp.83–90.

Bell, L. 'The new Public Record Office at Kew', in *JSA*, 5 no. 1 (1974), pp.1–7.

Bell, L and Faye, B. *La conception des bâtiments d'archives en pays tropical* (Unesco, Paris 1979).

Benoit, G. 'Pour ou contre l'utilisation des bâtiments anciens pour les archives', in *Janus*, 1992.1, pp.52–7.

Bish, T. *The care of business records* (Business Archives Council, Record Aids no 7, 1986).

Boss, RW. 'Collection security', in *Library Trends*, Summer 1984, pp.39–48.

British Standards Institution. *British standard recommendations for storage and exhibition of archival documents* (BS 5454: 1989).

Buchmann, W. 'Der Neubau für das Bundesarchiv in Koblenz', in *Archivum*, XXXI (1986), pp.27–36.

Buchmann, W. 'Planning an archive building: the cooperation between architect and archivist', in *Archive buildings and the conservation of archival material* (Mitteilungen des Österreichischen Staatsarchivs, 39, Vienna 1986), pp.202–17 [a revised version of a paper in German printed in *Archivum* 31 (1986)].

Burke, RB and Adeloye, S. *A manual of basic museum security* (ICOM/ICMS, 1986).

[Chubb leaflet]. 'How to protect the ozone layer' (1990).

Cobb, HS. 'The Victoria Tower and the Records of Parliament 1864–1986', in *The Table*, 54 (1986), pp.54–63.

Collis, IP. 'The ideal layout of a local record repository', in *Archives*, I no 6, pp.31–5 (1951) and no 7, pp.52–9 (1952).

Cox, N. 'The new Public Record Office at Kew', in *Archivum*, 31 (1986), pp.133–42.

Cunningham, JKH. 'The protection of records and documents against fire', in *JSA*, 3 no. 8 (October 1968), pp.411–17.

Daniels, V. 'Air pollution and the archivist', in *JSA*, 6 no. 3 (April 1979), pp.154–6.

Department of the Environment. *Environmental action guide for building and purchasing managers* (HMSO, 1991).

Department of the Environment. *Fire fighting. Protecting the ozone layer and safeguarding your business* (1992).

Department of the Environment: Property Services Agency. *Fire precautions guide* (1987).

Dewe, M (ed). *Library buildings: preparation for planning* (IFLA publications no 48, 1989).

Duchein, M. *Archive buildings and equipment*, (ICA handbooks series, vol. 6, 2nd revised and enlarged edn. ed. Walne, P., translated by Thomas, D., 1988).

Duchein, M. 'Les bâtiments d'archives départementales en France', in *Archivum*, 6 (1956), pp.108–76.

Duchein, M. *Les rayonnages d'archives* (Centre d'information du matériel et des articles de bureau: supplement to Bulletin, June 1967, Paris).

Ede, JR. 'Steel shelving for record storage', in *JSA*, 2 no 3 (April 1961), pp.114–19.

Energy, Department of. *Energy efficiency in buildings: libraries, museums and churches* (Energy Efficiency Office, 1990).

Faber, O and Kell, JR [originators]. *Heating and air-conditioning of buildings* (6th revised edn by Kell, JR and Martin, PL, 1979).

Faulkner-Brown, H. 'Planning and designing library buildings – the tuition of architects', in Dewe, *Library buildings*, pp.49–62.

Faulkner-Brown, H. 'Protecting the library against fire: some considerations affecting interior layout and design', in Fuhlrott and Dewe (1982).

Faye, B. 'The design of archive buildings', in *Unesco Journal of Information Science, Librarianship and Archives Administration*, IV (1982), pp.88–93.

Forde, H. 'Setting up a conservation workshop', in *Library Conservation News*, 35 (April 1992), pp.3, 6).

France: Direction des Archives, *Bâtiments d'archives. Vingt ans d'architecture française 1965–1985*, (Paris, 1986).

France: Direction des Archives. *Manuel d'archivistique* (1970), especially part III chapter I, 'Les bâtiments et installations des archives'.

Fuhlrott, R and Dewe, M. *Library interior layout and design* (IFLA publications no 24, 1982).

Gondos, V jr. 'American archival architecture', in *Bulletin of the American Institute of Architects*, Sept 1947, pp.27–32.

Gondos, V jr. 'Archival buildings – programming and planning', in *American Archivist*, 27 no. 4 (1964), pp.467–83.

Gondos, V jr. *Reader for archives and records center buildings*, (Society of American Archivists: committee on archival buildings and equipment, 1970).

Gray, V. 'The County Record Office: the unfolding of an idea', in K Neale (ed), *An Essex tribute: essays presented to Frederick G Emmison* (1987), pp.11–25.

[Guidelines for record repositories: see below, Royal Commission on Historical Manuscripts].

Hackney, S. 'The distribution of gaseous air pollution within museums', in *Studies in Conservation*, 29 (1984), pp.105–116.

Hallam Smith, E. 'Illuminating records', in *Museums Journal*, February 1992, pp.38–9.

Harrison, KC (ed). *Public library buildings 1975–1983* (1987).

Harrison, KC (ed). *Library buildings 1984–1989* (1990).

Haymond, J. 'Adaptive reuse of old buildings for archives', in *American Archivist*, 45 no. 1, (1982), pp.11–18.

Hedar, S. 'On building archives', in *Archivum*, 6 (1956), pp.83–7.

Hirst, R. *Underdown's practical fire protection* (3rd edn, 1989).

Hoare, N. *Security for museums* (Committee for Area Museum Councils/Museums Association, 1990).

Huws, D. 'The National Library of Wales: a building and its adaptation', in Dewe, *Library buildings*, pp.88–101.

[INLOGOV, see Norton, Serjeant].

Jones, DR. 'A stable future for Suffolk's archives', in *Storage: preprints for UKIC conference Restoration '91* (1991).

Keene, JA and Roper, M. *Planning, equipping and staffing a document reprographic service*, (Unesco RAMP study, Paris 1984, PGI-84/WS/8).

Kitching, CJ. 'BS 5454: a commentary on the revised edition', in *JSA*, 10 no. 3 (1989), pp.99–102.

Konya, A. *Libraries: a briefing and design guide* (Architectural Press, Briefing and Design Guides, 1986).

Langwell, WH. 'Measurement of the effects of air pollution on paper documents', in *JSA*, 5 no. 6 (1976), pp.372–3.

Lee, S. 'National Library of Scotland – protecting a nation's heritage' [sprinkler system], in *Fire Prevention*, 249 (May 1992), pp.22–6.

[London School of Economics]. *LSE: the new library* (1978).

McIntyre, DA. *Indoor climate* (1980).

Mason, E. *Mason on library buildings* (1980).

Mason, P. 'Archival security: new solutions to an old problem', in *The American Archivist*, 38 (1975), pp.477–92.

Morris, J. *Managing the library fire risk* (2nd edn, Berkeley 1979).

Morris, J. 'Protecting the library from fire', in *Library Trends*, 33 (1984), pp.49–56.

Nicol, A. 'Archival buildings: purpose-built or converted', in Norton [see below] pp.19–22.

Norton, A (ed.). *Archives in '86* (INLOGOV, Birmingham, 1986), pp.19–22.

Occupational Health Service. *Standards for a healthy indoor environment* (OHS Briefing Note no 1, 3rd edn, April 1990).

Padfield, T. 'The control of relative humidity and air pollution in showcases and picture frames', in *Studies in Conservation*, 11 (1966), p.8.

Pascoe, MW. *Impact of environmental pollution on the preservation of archives and records: a RAMP study* (Unesco, Paris 1988 PGI-88/WS/18).

Pescador del Hoyo, M del Carmen. *El archivo: instalación y conservación* (Madrid, 1988).

Plenderleith, HJ and Werner, AEA. *The conservation of antiquities and works of art: treatment, repair and restoration* (2nd edn, 1971).

Porges, F. *Handbook of heating, ventilating and air-conditioning* (8th edn., 1982).

[Public Record Office]. 'The Public Record Office, Kew: structural and mechanical solutions to the fire protection of irreplaceable documents', in *Fire Prevention*, 125 (June 1978), pp.16–19.

Ratcliffe, FW. 'Preparing for the planning and design of a library building', in Dewe, *Library buildings*, pp.13–28.

Reimann, N. 'The communal system of record offices in Germany at the beginning of the nineties', in *Janus*, 1991.1, pp.54–66.

Roper, M. 'Advanced technical media: the conservation and storage of audio-visual and machine-readable records', in *JSA*, 7 no 2 (October 1982) pp.106–12.

Roper, M. *Planning, equipping and staffing an archival preservation and conservation service* (Unesco RAMP study, Paris 1989, PGI-89/WS/4).

Royal Commission on Historical Manuscripts. *A standard for record repositories on constitution and finance, staffing, acquisition and access* (1990). [Guidelines for record repositories issued by the Public

Record Office, the Commission and the Scottish Record Office (1989) appear as an appendix]. Reprinted in *JSA*, 12 no 2 (Autumn 1991), pp.114–22.

Schellenberg, TR. 'Modern archival buildings', in *Archivum*, 6 (1956) pp.88–92.

Serjeant, W. 'Archives in the 80s: overview I', in Norton, A (ed.), *Archives in the eighties* (INLOGOV, Birmingham, 1984), pp.5–14.

Shepilova, IG. *Main principles of fire protection in libraries and archives* (Unesco RAMP study, Paris 1992, PGI-92/WS/14).

Shepilova, IG. 'Protection of documents in special archives buildings' (typescript of a paper given at the ICA committee on archive buildings and equipment, Vienna 1990).

Shields, TJ and Silcock, GWH. *Buildings and fire* (1987).

Simonet, JE. 'Protection against theft and burglary in archive buildings' (typescript of paper given at the ICA Committee on Archive Buildings and Equipment, Vienna 1990; subsequently printed, in French, in *Janus*, 1992.1, pp.101–105).

Simonet, JE. 'Security in old buildings fitted out for archives: theft and vandalism' (typescript of paper given at the ICA Committee on Archive Buildings and Equipment, Turin 1989; subsequently printed, in French, in *Janus*, 1992.1, pp.62–8).

Smith, BS. 'Record repositories in 1984', in *JSA*, 8 no 1 (April 1986), pp.1–16.

Society of Archivists. 'Towards a national policy for archives' (1983).

Stazicker, E. 'Climatic control: a hopeless bewilderment?', in *JSA*, 8 no.3 (April 1987), pp.171–3.

Stehkaemper, H. ' "Natural" air-conditioning of stacks', in *Restaurator*, 9 no 4 (1988), pp.163–177. [A translated and expanded version of ' "Natürliche" Magazinklimatisierung', in *Der Archivar*, 26 (1973), coll.450–62].

Stewart, WJ. 'Creating a secure archives' (typescript of a paper given at the ICA committee on archive buildings and equipment, Vienna 1990).

Storey, R., Wherry, AM., and Wilson, JF. 'Three views on security', in *JSA*, 10 (1989), pp.108–14'.

Thomas, DL. 'Architectural design and technical equipment for the physical protection and conservation of documents', in *Mitteilungen des Österreichischen Staatsarchivs*, 39 (1986), pp.233–51.

Thomas, DL. 'Archive buildings: international

comparisons', in *JSA*, 9 no.1 (January 1988), pp.38–44.

Thomas, DL. 'Security at the new Public Record Office', in *Janus*, 1992.1, pp.110–15.

Thomas, DL. *Study on control of security and storage of holdings* (Unesco RAMP study, Paris 1986, PGI-86/WS/23).

Thompson, A. *Library buildings of Britain and Europe* (1963).

Thomson, G. 'Air pollution – a review for conservation chemists', in *Studies in Conservation*, 10 (1965), pp.145–67.

Thomson, G. 'Annual exposure to light within museums', in *Studies in Conservation*, 12 (1967), pp.26–35.

Thomson, G. 'Relative humidity variation with temperature in a case containing wood', in *Studies in Conservation*, 9 (1964), pp.153–69.

Thomson, G. 'Stabilization of relative humidity in exhibition cases: hygrometric half time', in *Studies in Conservation*, 22 (1977), pp.85–105.

Thomson, G. *The museum environment* (2nd edn, 1986).

Tillotson, RG. *Museum security* (ICOM, Paris 1977).

Tong, D. 'Sick building syndrome', in *New Consumer*, 2 (1989/90), pp.24–5.

[Underdown, *see* Hirst].

Voronin, I. 'La construction des bâtiments d'archives en URSS', in *Archivum*, 7 (1957), pp.3–9.

Walch, T. *Archives & manuscripts: security* (Society of American Archivists Basic Manuals Series, Chicago 1977, revised 1980).

Walsh, T. 'Air conditioning for archives', in *Archives and Manuscripts*, 8 no 2 (1980), pp.70–78.

Ward, A. *A manual of sound archive administration* (1990).

Warren, PR. 'The Public Record Office, Kew – indoor air quality' [unpublished typescript, 1984].

Wherry, AM. 'Security and the public', in Norton, A (ed.) *Bringing archives closer to the public* (Association of County Archivists/INLOGOV, 1988).

[Wherry, AM: see also Storey].

Woods, C. 'Designing a conservation room: an example from Dorset', in *JSA*, 13 no.2, (Autumn 1992), pp.132–5.

Part 2
Case studies

The aim of this second part of the volume is to present short illustrated descriptions of a sample of the new archive buildings of this period, chosen to give a broad impression of the different kinds of building encountered in the course of the study: large and small, purpose-built and converted. An attempt has also been made to reflect the range of parent authorities which have sponsored them, and to offer wide geographical coverage. Inclusion here, therefore, does not necessarily indicate that a building is of a higher standard than one which, for reasons of space and economy alone, has had to be omitted from this selection. A checklist of all the buildings taken into account is given in the Appendix, where references are cited to published articles about some of the buildings not featured among the case studies.

BBC Written Archives Centre

Berkshire Record Office

Cheshire Record Office

Cornwall Record Office

Cumbria Record Office, Barrow

Doncaster Archives Department

Dorset County Record Office

Dumfries Archive Centre

East Sussex Record Office

Glasgow University Archives Business Records Centre

Greater Manchester County Record Office

Gwynedd Archives and Museums Service: Caernarfon Area Record Office

Hammersmith and Fulham Archives

Hampshire Record Office

Hereford and Worcester Record Office: County Hall, Worcester

Lancashire Record Office

Lincolnshire Archives

Museum of Science and Industry in Manchester

National Film Archive: J Paul Getty Jr Conservation Centre

National Library of Wales

Northamptonshire Record Office

North Devon Record Office, Barnstaple

North Yorkshire County Record Office

Nottinghamshire Archives

Post Office Archives

Public Record Office

Sheffield Archives

Southampton University Library: Archives and special collections

Suffolk Record Office

West Sussex Record Office

BBC Written Archives Centre

Caversham Park, Reading
British Broadcasting Corporation
Purpose-built archive store and conversion of offices, 1990

On a sensitive site for development, between a school and playing fields, and facing suburban houses, the new BBC Written Archives Centre (concept design by David Hallahan of the BBC's Architect's Department, detail design and construction by Shepherd Construction Ltd) has been crafted to blend in with its domestic surroundings and, so far as possible, to reflect their scale. The grounds have been thoughtfully landscaped for year-round colour with gardens, lawns, trees and shingle paths, and even the occasional bird box and bench, and the main pedestrian entrance incorporates a wrought-iron garden gate in memory of CH Middleton, the radio gardening expert.

The core of the development is the original 1920s bungalow of the matron of a sanatorium built adjacent to Caversham Park, and the main single-storey block of the sanatorium to the rear, which first came to house the Written Archives in 1970, with the yard between the two roofed over and converted into a general office. By the late 1980s the archives had spilled over into numerous portakabins on the site, and redevelopment became a pressing need.

The bungalow (which had formerly housed a search room and staff offices) and the main block were retained in the 1990 redevelopment. The old general office was converted into a new search room, and to the side and rear in place of the portakabins a large purpose-built single-storey repository was added, allowing the original block to be adapted as an open-plan work room for ten staff, with other new amenities including a larger staff common room and a WC for the disabled. The opportunity was taken to re-roof the original buildings, upgrade the central heating system, and enclose the original verandah on the south wall to create a passage through the building without crossing the reading room.

The street frontage of the new block, discreetly set back from the line of the bungalow, has been given domestic scale by equipping the document reception area with a homely front door and windows (functionally not strictly necessary) and by giving the plant room louvred vents of dark stained wood and a brick chimney. The low-sweeping roofs (four successive pitches, one behind the other), covered in grey reconstituted slates on timber battens, overhang the walls by a metre or so all round, carried on a colonnade of wooden pillars rising from a shingle path on a hardcore sub base. A high thermal inertia design was ruled out on grounds of initial cost, but elements of the technique have been employed. The cavity wall comprises an inner wall of concrete blockwork, with an external wall of red facing bricks. The roof space is substantially insulated, and ventilated through louvres in the gable ends, with access to all roof areas by walkways in the roof space. Mechanically-assisted ventilation, operating round the clock, controls temperature and relative humidity, and a new gas-fired central heating system serves the whole complex. The architect, building contractor and shelving manufacturer worked together to plan the use of space and ensure minimum disruption to the mobile racking from the siting of pillars. A small extension on the north side of the repository block has been designed to house two rooms which can be separately controlled, one for more important or sensitive documents, and the other for the few non-paper media held by the centre, including microfilm masters. The building is protected throughout by fire- and intruder-detectors.

Cost: £1.25 million.

Storage area: 14,000 sq ft/39,000 linear ft.

Berkshire Record Office

Shinfield Park, Reading
Berkshire County Council
Purpose-built within shire hall, 1980

When the new shire hall on the outskirts of Reading was conceived in the late 1970s it incorporated a purpose-designed record office. It was one of the last county record offices to be built within the administrative headquarters of its parent authority, against the recent trend towards free-standing buildings, and is the only one of its kind featured in this volume.

The site, on a hillside above the M4, although three miles from the town centre, is well served by buses. The plentiful glazing of the exterior of the whole building is quickly forgotten in the austerity of the record office cocooned in the interior, entirely surrounded by other functions and having no outside walls and therefore no windows: not only in the storage area but also in the search room, staff offices and conservation workshop. The brick perimeter walls which demarcate the record office have thick steel fire doors at all points of entry and exit, reinforcing the overall fortress-like impression.

This has both strengths and weaknesses. Security and protection against fire are of a high standard, with the plant room off site, the main electrical installations isolated outside the strongroom, intruder- and fire-detectors and an automatic carbon dioxide fire-extinction system. But the record office is entirely dependent upon the building's air-conditioning system and power supply for all air and light. The air-handling plant has not always maintained steady temperature and relative humidity within the recommended limits, but the worst local problems have been overcome by installing powerful fans and mesh (instead of solid) end-panels to the mobile racking to improve air circulation. The strongrooms, which are of a convenient size and open-plan but of a curiously irregular shape for a purpose-designed building, occupy a semi-basement down a flight of steps five feet below the level of the search room, which makes for inconveniences in producing records, although a rarely-used book-lift is provided.

The public search room is comfortably appointed, but can cater for only some 16 readers of records and 14 of microfilm at a time. Its multi-functional nature, incorporating reference desk, finding aids, microfilm readers and a large map table in addition to conventional study tables, is on occasion a source of noise and distraction in such a small space.

The ground-plan lacks corridors, with the result that several of the interconnected rooms have to be used as through routes. Although the planned functions of some smaller rooms have been progressively changed over time to assist the flow of work and provide an acceptable working temperature for staff, no satisfactory solution has been found to

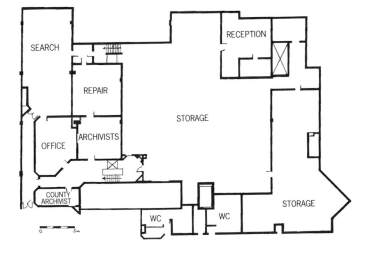

the provision of staff offices and work-rooms of a size appropriate to the tasks in hand, and space is everywhere at a premium. The building lacks any lecture or seminar room and a staff room. A new record office is now under consideration.

Cost: not separately costed.

Storage: 4,500 linear metres.

Cheshire Record Office

Duke Street, Chester
Cheshire County Council
Converted warehouse, 1985

By good fortune, at a time when Cheshire County Council was anxious to take over for other purposes the space in Chester Castle formerly occupied by the record office, and a number of alternative sites had already proved unsatisfactory, a convenient site became available in Duke Street only some 400 yards from County Hall, offering a building that was already well adapted both for storage and public uses, most recently used by Sothebys as a warehouse and auction room.

Originating in the mid nineteenth century as a warehouse, from the 1870s to the 1970s it was Messrs Brown's Chester and N Wales Furniture Repository. It comprises four inter-connected brick-built blocks enclosing a central courtyard. This layout enhances physical and

environmental security by separating off the public services and enabling power and environmental systems to be matched to the individual requirements of each block. There are no stairs to impede horizontal communications, and the warehouse lift has been a notable asset.

The building, however, required substantial alteration to bring it up to the standard of BS 5454. This was undertaken in two phases. The principal storage block, of four storeys, had wooden floors supported on wooden beams and joists, which did not offer a sufficiently strong floor-loading capacity, and also dictated specially stringent fire precautions. New concrete foundations were laid, and a steel frame with steel girders and joists was introduced to support static steel racking arranged in bays off a central aisle. The racking is secured to the joists by means of steel studs protruding through the floor. An automatic halon fire-extinction system was installed, linked through an agency to the brigade. It was shown in a test to be capable of extinguishing a fire in 7 seconds.

Air-conditioning was ruled out on grounds of cost. As an alternative the windows in the storage block were bricked in and the roof thickly insulated to assist thermal inertia. With fans to circulate the air, and portable humidifiers for use when required, this has been found, after a few teething troubles, to maintain a stable climate.

In 1988/89 as additional funds became available the second storage block was developed to provide a further 3 floors of storage space. The block was gutted and new reinforced concrete floors inserted. The opportunity was taken to insert an air-circulation system on each floor.

The austere street face of the warehouse is somewhat lightened by the addition of coats of arms of the county and diocese, whilst plants introduced into the courtyard in tubs have provided a more welcoming approach. The building has enabled the record office to consolidate its holdings, other than modern records, on one site, and to provide a pleasant working environment for both staff and public, with space for 14 readers of original material and 15 of microfilm, together with exhibition space and a public meeting room.

Cost:
  phase 1: approximately £700,000.
  phase 2: approximately £180,000.

Storage: 861.7 cubic metres.

Published reference:
FI Dunn, 'The new Cheshire Record Office: a nineteenth-century warehouse', in Norton (INLOGOV 1986).

Cornwall Record Office

County Hall, Truro
Cornwall County Council
Purpose-built, 1964; extended 1974, 1983, 1988

Cornwall Record Office, established in 1951 in the wing of a private house, pitched a base camp for a new record office in the grounds of county hall in 1964. It was a too economical single-storey structure of concrete block, containing only two of the four strongrooms originally planned. The other two were added in the first extension in 1974. Although this is a sloping, hill-top site, space has been found for two further extensions in the period covered by this survey, and the building is now planned to suffice until about 2001, when a fourth and final extension is contemplated.

The 1983 extension added further strongrooms, but still left several functions uncomfortably cramped both for staff and public. The most recent development doubled the size of the search room and gave it a new façade of attractive, openable windows with wooden frames in keeping with the surrounding park-like campus which provides a restful and quiet environment some five minutes' walk from the railway station. The room, which is multi-functional in containing all the reference services, has seating for 20 readers of records and 12 of microfiche and is free of columns and obstructions, giving good sight-lines for invigilation. A staff counter, for registration of new readers and professional assistance, is separated from the issue and return desk which provides a second point of invigilation.

Security, too, was upgraded in 1988, with smoke-detectors and intruder-detectors and alarms throughout. The staff offices were extended and re-designed, with a new, amply-windowed conservation workshop and a system of 'flexi-space' (in effect shared desks) to maximise the use of space in a still economical layout.

The strongrooms, now air-conditioned, lie either side of a spinal corridor entered from a staff-only area. The doors are fitted with fusible links to close automatically in the event of a fire. With the installation of mobile racking in three of the rooms (and planned for another), and

the introduction of a computer-controlled document management system, the opportunity has been taken to shelve many records by type and size in order to economise on storage space. A separate room for maps has its own custom-built racking.

The most recent extension, which also involved the adaptation of the existing building, was not without its problems. The siting of steel roof girders and wiring prevented implementation of the plans as originally conceived. Uncertainty over the amount of space which would be required above the racking to accommodate the air-conditioning trunking made planning for the shelving difficult. The use of space heaters in the offices and search room also proved problematic in restricting wall space. But the record office has surmounted these difficulties and is now well up to the standards expected in the 1990s.

Storage: 330 cubic metres.

Published reference:
David E Ival, 'Cornwall record office', in *Family Tree*, May 1988, p.28.

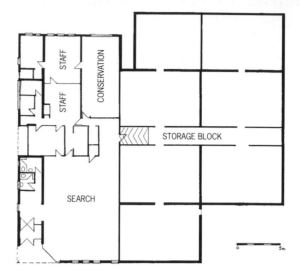

Cumbria Record Office, Barrow

Duke Street, Barrow-in-Furness
Cumbria County Council
Purpose-built, 1976–78, in two phases

It was no easy matter to find a suitable site for a branch of the Cumbria Archive Service to serve Furness and take in the local government records held in Barrow town hall when Furness was detached from Lancashire in 1974. Several buildings including a church were considered for conversion, and for a while from 1975 former Gas offices at Dalton in Furness temporarily housed the incipient service until a more permanent solution was found for a purpose-built record office on a former school playground adjacent to the Central Library on Ramsden Square, Barrow, conveniently central in relation to bus and railway stations. It opened to the public in January 1979.

The site was not without its problems. The library on one side and houses and streets on the others defined the limits of the development. The nature and location as well as cost constraints and the uncertainty of the load-bearing capacity of the ground beside an underground watercourse, the Hindpool, dictated a modest, single-storey building which is now uncomfortably full.

Constructed (in two phases) of reinforced concrete blocks and faced throughout in red brick, the building has a flat roof, also of reinforced concrete over the storage areas, which although insulated and covered in asphalt has not been immune from leaks. Good use has been made of a compact assemblage of rectangular rooms, both to maximise the use of space for all functions and to enable the building to be managed and the readers supervised by a necessarily small number of staff. The strongrooms are fitted with mobile racking. The two staff offices have windows into the search room to enhance invigilation. Among the few awkward points of the design, the loading bay door, which serves both the library and the record office, requires a sharp 90 degree turn for incoming records and does not give immediate access to a secure area.

As one of the first archive buildings to be purpose built after the publication of BS 5454:1977, this incorporates security, fire-detection and full air-conditioning broadly in line with the Standard. Consideration was being given during this survey to upgrading these services.

Cost: figure not available.

Storage: *c.* 5,000 linear ft.

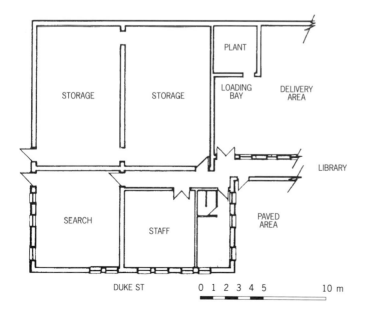

Doncaster Archives Department

Balby, Doncaster
Doncaster Metropolitan Borough Council
Converted schools, 1982–3; 1985

Until 1982 the public front of Doncaster's archive service was in a branch library, but with some records accommodated off-site. The conversion in two phases, first of a former junior school to serve as an archives building with storage, research and office facilities (1982), and secondly of an adjacent infants school as a modern records centre (1985), has transformed the service and streamlined its entire operation.

The main building (1904), a mile from the town centre, has been described by the archivist as 'single storey, solidly constructed of brick, stone and substantial timbers with steeply pitched slate roofs, networks of valley gutters and large expanses of glazing'. The valley gutters, characteristic of school buildings of this period, are a potential design weakness, and have here been a cause of superficial fabric damage by rainwater on several occasions.

The school hall, together with one classroom at each end of it, was converted into a single secure strongroom of 2,400 sq ft, fitted with mobile steel racking to provide in all some 5,338 linear feet of storage. New internal walls were built to create a corridor separating the central hall from the classrooms which had originally opened directly on to it. A false ceiling was introduced, with additional insulation above, to mitigate the effects of the hall's 24ft height on the internal environment. With partial air-conditioning, temperature and relative humidity are controlled to meet the recommendations of BS 5454. Although the floor was strong enough to support mobile racking, it proved to be uneven, and the tracks had to be laid on ramps which impede the passage of trolleys.

Relatively little construction work was required to adapt the main range of six classrooms, each of some 600 sq ft, into a searchroom for 12 readers, a meeting room and offices leaving, at least initially, some additional space to be used by the council's graphics department. But one penalty of minimum interference with the existing structure is that the areas and height of the rooms bear no relation to the specific functions they are required to serve. The large, high windows which may have been ideal for school use let in too much direct sunlight for the good of records in the searchroom and have had to be covered with blinds and an anti-ultra-violet film. The budget has proved insufficient to provide for all the necessary maintenance and decoration, but both buildings are equipped with smoke- and intruder-detection systems. The former wash rooms and miscellaneous small rooms on the opposite side of the building have not been seen as suitable for adaptation for long-term use, and serve at best for reception and temporary storage.

Cost: figure not available.

Storage: 5,338 linear ft.

Published reference:
B Barber, 'The Doncaster Metropolitan Borough Archive Department', in *Archives*, XIX no 83 (April 1990), pp.115–120.

Dorset County Record Office

Bridport Road, Dorchester
Dorset County Council
Converted Regimental Association building with substantial additions and a purpose-built repository, 1991

The new record office in Dorchester (by Hubbard Ford in association with the county architect), although incorporating an older building on the site, has been developed by new building to the sides and rear in such a way that the whole building appears new from the street front. The large open site, adjoining the main road towards Bridport and flanked by a branch railway line in a cutting, is ringed by other public buildings, including regimental museum, postal sorting office, crown offices and county council offices.

The free-standing two-storey record office building of red brick is conceived as two linked blocks: public rooms at ground level at the front with staff offices and conservation and reprographics workshops above; and storage in a new purpose-built block of red and buff brick

at the rear, with space for an estimated 25–30 years' accessions.

Public facilities have been improved beyond recognition compared with those in the cramped premises of the earlier record office on the County Hall site. A staffed reception area, with space for coats and bags, gives access respectively to the public search rooms, a small common room, and a generously large exhibition room with lecture room beyond. The exhibition room – a model of its kind – has been fitted with display boards of painted blockboard extending from floor to ceiling, standing clear of the walls but anchored to them. The windows, here as elsewhere in the building, are openable, double-glazed and of strengthened glass, screened against ultraviolet light and fitted with adjustable blinds. Tracked lighting is controlled on

dimmer switches. Double doors from this room into the lecture room can be opened to allow greater circulation space for receptions. The lecture room, which has excellent acoustics, can seat 30 comfortably at tables and up to 100 with chairs only. Closed-circuit television, monitored from the reception desk, is used in both these rooms to enhance security. Extractor fans assist ventilation as necessary.

The search area, divided into three separate rooms for consultation respectively of catalogues, microfilm (29 readers) and original records (42 readers), is serviced and invigilated from a central staff counter. The main search room, without columns, has good sight-lines for invigilation, and in addition the assistant county archivist's office overlooks the room through a glazed panel.

The staff offices, to which admittance from the exterior is by means of pass cards and combination locks, have been conceived as far as possible to allow for some expansion in complement over the next two to three decades and to be adaptable to changes of structure. They are well appointed and generously provided with natural light, some by means of a light-well in the centre of the building. Electrical and computer cabling ducts are carried in the walls at desk height. Facilities include a common room, sick bay and shower. The purpose-designed conservation workshop is separately described on p.67. Adjacent to it is a suite of rooms for reprographics, including camera rooms and a dark room.

The windowless repository block on two floors incorporates features of high thermal inertia, with an insulated cavity wall (interior concrete block, exterior brick), and a sharply overhanging roof. But the repository is also provided with three distinct air-handling systems to climatise respectively the main storage area, a separate film store where cooler and less humid conditions are required, and the conservation workshop (one of the few in the country to be fully air-conditioned). The system is computer-controlled and its performance logged also by computer. The repository is equipped with a halon automatic fire-extinguishing system and (like the rest of the building) with smoke- and intruder-detectors. Insufficient space was allowed in the initial plans for the air-handling plant as finally conceived, and eventually there was no alternative to locating it in the roof space over the upper repository. With careful precautions, including tanking and externally draining the whole area and installing smoke and water alarms, something of a virtue has been made of this necessity.

Cost: £2.25 million.

Storage: 1,578 cubic metres.

Dumfries Archive Centre

Burns Street, Dumfries
Nithsdale District Council
Converted house, 1986

This two-storey stone-built house, with a small single-storey extension at one side, used to be home to the curator of the Burns House museum immediately across the road. In 1986 it was earmarked as the new repository for the district archives, and it was opened in 1987, enabling collections from a number of different sites to be brought under one roof. There are plans to build a second storey over the existing extension and adjacent shed, but even this substantial gain in storage space will still leave the Centre the smallest of the buildings covered in the present survey. Its size, however, is by no means proportional to its significance within the framework of local authority provision for archives in Scotland.

Few alterations were made to the basic layout of the house. The small kitchen has been retained for staff use and doubles as a photocopying room; the bath has been removed from the bathroom (downstairs) to make additional general storage space. The two upstairs bedrooms (approached by very steep stairs which were one of the factors determining that the building should not revert to conventional domestic use) and the principal room to the right of the front door downstairs were fitted out with static racking which very quickly filled up, and the single-storey annexe was developed as a search room, although it can seat no more than eight readers at once.

Security was considerably upgraded, with intruder-alarms and smoke-detectors fitted to doors and windows. The surroundings are well lit at night by the large spotlight (visible in the illustration) trained from here on to Burns House.

The first archivist was appointed in 1987, and in recognition of its achievement in giving the archives a higher public profile the Centre won the research prize in the Museum of the Year Award for Scotland in 1988, the only record repository so far to achieve this distinction.

Published references:
Marion M Stewart's articles on the Centre, in the *Dumfries and Galloway Family History Society Newsletters* 1987.

Marion M Stewart, 'The Dumfries Archive Centre', in *Scottish Record Office Newsletter*, 8 (Spring 1988), pp.7–8.

East Sussex Record Office

Castle Precinct, Lewes
East Sussex County Council
Converted maltings, 1983

The Maltings, a fine flint and brick structure on a prominent site next to the curtain wall of Lewes castle, was built in 1852 for the Castle brewery, and sold shortly afterwards to the Beard family, brewers. In 1947 it became a builders' merchants store, and when eventually purchased by the county council in 1968 it was a store for school furniture.

Plans for its conversion into a record office were first drawn up in 1973, but shelved owing to local government restructuring and tight constraints on expenditure. The idea seemed too good to waste, and a new scheme was drawn up in 1981. But since then the record office has had to soldier on through one of the longest-running phased conversions, with continuous reliance on out-stores.

The Maltings was listed as a building of historic importance in 1985. It originally comprised a large rectangular storage area on a single level but overlooked by a wooden gallery carried on wooden beams with cast iron pillars; at one end were two circular kilns and a yard; and at the other a number of offices, with further accommodation on the first floor extending the full length of the building.

The first stage of occupancy, involving the record office's conservation and modern records departments (though neither of them in the premises designated for their use in the full scheme) began in 1976. But only a modest amount of shelving was then made available for archival storage, on the galleries. In 1981 the modern records operation moved out to a warehouse on an industrial estate, freeing a substantial amount of storage space at the Maltings but without the resources to exploit it immediately.

Over the next two years a boiler room, heating system and document hoist were installed, and then a search room, map room and offices were established and additional racking fitted, although still well short of both the building's capacity and the record office's needs.

Public services moved from the record office's original headquarters in (17th-century) Pelham House to the new search room at the Maltings in 1983. Additional racking was acquired in 1985. But it was 1988 before-the 'first phase' of the conversion was truly completed by filling in the space between the galleries to create a mezzanine floor, and installing mobile racking below and static above. During 1991/92 further work was planned to convert the kilns and yard into a microfilm reading room and a new conservation workshop, to free the former workshop for conversion into a lecture room. When this work is completed, probably in the mid 1990s, the building will at last be functioning as originally conceived.

Cash has not been the only constraint. The great quantities of wood in the internal structure of the building have given rise to concern both on account of the fire risk (against which stringent precautions have been taken including the installation of smoke-detectors linked to the fire brigade) and also because of the intrusion of massive low beams at regular intervals in the storage space, and generally low headroom throughout. On its first occupancy parts of the upper floor were found to suffer extremes of heat in summer, but chilling units have now solved the problem. Even with the completion of the development it has not proved possible to accommodate under one roof all the record office's archival holdings, and there is no further room for extension on the site. On the other hand it has enabled the record office to maintain its presence in the town centre, and in a building of some distinction.

This example highlights both some of the strengths and some of the weaknesses of converted historic buildings. Above all it emphasises the difficulties which can be experienced if, for whatever reason, it is not found practicable to go ahead with the full plan at the outset. Had the building been fully developed as planned in 1973 it would by now have had 20 years of occupancy – which is the full projected life span of some of the buildings described in this volume.

Storage: 6,350 linear ft excluding maps.

Glasgow University Archives Business Records Centre

Thurso Street, Glasgow
University of Glasgow
Converted flour mill, 1989

This five-storey brick building near Kelvin Hall, with concrete frame and floors, began life as a flour mill and served for a time as a horse tram depot. It is now occupied by various departments of the university, with the vehicles and supplies departments respectively on the ground and first floors, the Business Records Centre on the second and third, and a library store on the fourth.

Its conversion in 1989 greatly increased the storage capacity of the University Archives, although the space has rapidly filled up. It is a sympathetic use for a retired industrial building, a number of whose existing features marked it out as ripe for conversion: a loading bay and stout lift, reasonable load-bearing floors

(although not up to mobile racking), comparatively few windows and, above all, large storage areas (when inherited partitions had been removed and new internal walls of concrete block installed to demarcate the various new functions).

Conversion was not without its challenges. The structural columns somewhat restricted the layout of shelving. The overall floor plan had to fit round a central void which had housed the grain hoppers. The uneven concrete floors had to be screeded and sealed. And until essential maintenance had been undertaken there were some early problems of damp penetrating the external brickwork. But these teething troubles have now been successfully overcome, and the Centre has settled into a busy routine.

Public access is up two rather bleak and forbidding flights of stone stairs, but the search room, which seats about 10 readers, is comfortably furnished and has a small library of essential reference books. It is separated by a double-glazed partition from the adjacent staff office. On the same level are the document reception area (served by the lift from the loading bay at ground level), and the first of the two storage areas, the other being on the floor above.

Special attention has been paid to security, with intruder- and smoke-detectors linked to the respective authorities. The incoming air is filtered and washed in accordance with BS 5454 as a precaution against atmospheric pollution, but the system lacks a chilling facility, which has caused some problems in summer. High density, easily adjustable static racking is employed to suit the very varying shapes and sizes of the records held.

Further development of the top floor is

foreseen for the longer term, which might perhaps allow for the union of the whole archives department on this one site, or at least for additional space for seminars and public meetings.

Cost: approx. £900,000.

Storage: 3,365 linear metres.

Published reference:
MS Moss. 'Business records in Scotland 1970–1990', in *Scottish Industrial History*, 11–13 (1990), pp.119–127.

Greater Manchester County Record Office

Marshall Street, New Cross, Manchester
Association of Greater Manchester Authorities
Former cotton warehouse/textile workshops, converted in phases from 1981 (opened 1983)

When this building was acquired by the then Greater Manchester County Council, the ground floor was occupied by Messrs Geddes and Berger, textile converters. The original main entrance is dominated by the name of Marsden, Harcombe & Co. Development of the accommodation for record office use has been phased, and responsibility for it passed to the Association of Greater Manchester Authorities after the abolition of the County Council in 1986.

Storage, security, fire and environmental controls, and the fabric itself, have been progressively upgraded. In 1987 the entire building finally came into the record office's possession, making this now a nicely self-contained unit. Although located in what the record office itself describes as an 'unprepossessing' area on the 'wrong' side of Piccadilly, it is only about ten minutes' walk from the city centre, and well served by buses and the new Metrolink trams.

The warehouse, with concrete floors and pillars and a small amount of internal breeze-block partitioning, offered ample floor-loading capacity. It is faced with brick, but only has a troughed metal deck roof, put up before the record office's occupancy after a fire which destroyed the third floor. The building comprises a semi-basement (its windows now bricked up), a 'ground' floor (actually up some steps, making awkward access for the

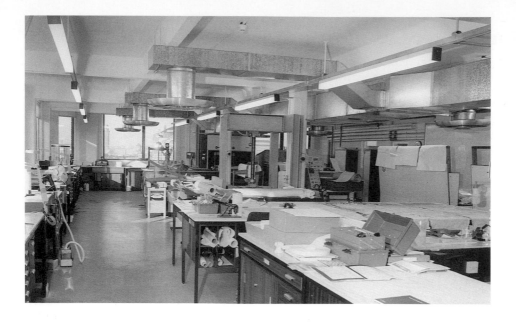

disabled), and first and second floors. The front of each floor is divided from the rear by a spinal fire corridor, which has proved useful in segregating storage from public and technical functions. A generous loading-bay at the rear (now protected by an electronically-operated steel roller door) and a goods lift were among the valuable assets inherited.

The original windows were of course designed to admit maximum sunlight. This was not ideal for an archive building, so they have been adapted and upgraded, fitted with tinted and filtered glass on the sides exposed most directly to the sun in the search room (first floor) and conservation workshop (second floor), and with those at lower levels protected by metal grilles against vandalism. Intruder-alarms have been installed.

In the most recent phase of development most of the building was provided with air-conditioning. The system is flexible enough to allow different temperature and relative humidity for different functions, including cool storage for photographs and film. But fitting such a system into a building like this which was not designed with air-conditioning in mind has not been entirely free of prob-

lems: the necessarily bulky trunking is a rather brooding presence, and the rush of air can be enough to rustle papers around in the workshop. A halon automatic fire-extinction system has been fitted, which (unusually) extends to the conservation workshop as well as to the storage areas.

The workshop, designed by a professional conservator, is (at some 3,000 sq ft) one of the largest and best-equipped of those studied for this volume. Its hardware includes a small freeze-drier which has already proved useful in rehabilitating water-damaged records from elsewhere. The search room is light, spacious and comfortable, and the clinical stairways which in former days were very much the staff entrance, have been brightened by a good coat of paint and a display of prints. Staff accommodation, although ample in total, is scattered around the different floors.

Cost: figure not available.

Storage: 910 cubic metres.

Published reference:
Family Tree, 3 no 4 (Feb 1987) p.18

Gwynedd Archives and Museums Service: Caernarfon Area Record Office

Victoria Dock, Caernarfon
Gwynedd County Council
Purpose-built, 1982

In December 1980 two major building projects were under way in Caernarfon: new county offices within the town, and a multi-storey car park on an old timber yard in the docks just outside the walls. The County Council had made no provision in their offices for the record office (then occupying disused gaol cells in the old complex). But realising that the car park would be an eyesore, especially from the sea, in what was fast becoming a maritime heritage area, it offered the county archivist a site for rapid development of a new repository in front of the car park. The building was completed in 1981 and opened in February 1982.

As a heritage exercise this was an unqualified success. From a distance the three-storey building resembles a brick warehouse (there are actually only a few courses of industrial brick) with a slate roof (laid on concrete slabs). The main structure is of concrete blocks supported by a steel frame. It is still flanked by working timber sheds. Small boats and the last Menai Strait ferry bob about in the sheltered waters in front. At the entrance to the dock is the Caernarfon Maritime Museum, a single-storey building refurbished in May 1981 to house a display related to the adjacent restored steam dredger. The Museum's secretary, Roy Wakeford, a member of the County Architect's staff, produced the design for the new record office, which blends almost too well into its surroundings: repeated requests for adequate signing have been turned down by the planners.

The repository is air-conditioned and protected by a halon automatic fire-extinction system. The risk of flood

damage has been minimised by raising the building on a plinth, with the public areas (exhibition space, sales point, education room and search room for 24 archive and 8 microfilm readers) on the ground floor, and the storage areas on the first and second floors. The pitched roof over the second floor strongroom was deliberately made high enough, and the troughed concrete floors designed to take a sufficient load, for a mezzanine floor to be inserted. This was under way in 1992/93, and should provide storage for a further twenty years. The staff offices on the ground and first floors all have magnificent views north-west over the harbour and the Menai Strait to Anglesey.

The disadvantages are mainly legacies of hasty planning and budgetary constraints in 1981. Not enough space was provided for ancillary activities: there is no public common room or staff tea room, no showers, no covered loading bay, little room for box storage. The ventilator shaft and toilets are awkwardly sited in the centre of the building, and the office and search room windows, opening outwards at the bottom, do not allow enough fresh air to circulate. No department leaving the old county offices was allowed new furniture, and the old shelving was accordingly transferred to the new building. Since then mobile shelving has been provided on the second floor (upgraded two years later on health and safety grounds by the addition of mechanised gearing), and additional funds have been set aside for mobile shelving throughout the new mezzanine floor.

Cost: £330,000.

Storage: 10,452 linear ft excluding mezzanine.

Hammersmith and Fulham Archives

The Lilla Huset, Hammersmith
London Borough of Hammersmith and Fulham
Purpose-built, 1992

Designed as an integral part of Ralph Erskine's striking London Ark project (Swedish developer Åke Larson), which towers above the Hammersmith flyover, the Lilla Huset ('little house') is a distinctive two-storey building faced in ornamental brick and copper. The archives department occupies the ground floor, whilst the first floor houses an urban studies centre and a business resource centre. A gallery area at this level is shared by all three.

The awkward shape of the site, between the busy Talgarth Road at one end and the railway line at the other, with the Ark

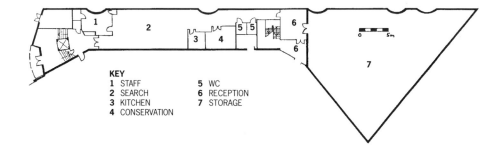

KEY
1 STAFF
2 SEARCH
3 KITCHEN
4 CONSERVATION
5 WC
6 RECEPTION
7 STORAGE

alongside, dictated a long, narrow building culminating in an almost triangular storage area with a sloping roof. In addition the architect planned the building around existing trees, by introducing occasional arcs of brick in otherwise straight walls. Additional landscaping has included bamboos and shrubs.

The search room is down a few steps from the public entrance, but there is a lift to assist access by the disabled. The room, which combines also the functions of local studies library and a museum/archives display area, accommodates 8 readers and a further 4 microform readers in comfort, with two staff desks. Double and triple glazing ensures a remarkably peaceful ambience even next to the main road. Doors, windows and other fittings have been finished to a high standard. As a deliberate feature of the design, pipes, girders and columns have been left exposed to view.

The small multi-purpose staff office has no exterior windows because plans for the future development of the adjacent land demanded that the main wall should be blind. There are, however, small internal windows on to the search room, and as a consolation the well-equipped staff room/kitchen, on the other side of

the building, facing the Ark, has plenty of natural light. This is true also of the small conservation workshop next to it.

The windowless strongroom, like the rest of the ground floor, is built of concrete blocks, with an insulated cavity and brick external cladding. The room is partially air-conditioned by means of wall-mounted heating/chilling units and externally-drained dehumidifiers. It is fitted partly with mobile and partly with static racking. This accommodation is a substantial improvement on the scattered storage and poor environmental controls of the Archives' previous premises, but the usable volume of space is less than the external dimensions might suggest owing to the shape, the structural supports and the sloping roof.

This could not be recommended as a practical standard design for a repository on a less encumbered site, but among small repositories it is certainly one of the most stylish, and will surely be the envy (in particular) of many other London borough archivists and their readers.

Cost: part of a larger development; figure not available.

Storage: *c*. 8,000 linear ft.

Hampshire Record Office (from 1993)

Sussex Street, Winchester
Hampshire County Council
Purpose-built, 1992/93

The new building for Hampshire Record Office is on a site immediately opposite the railway station. It was under construction in the course of this study and due to open in 1993.

The building, of strikingly original design, presents an outer face of traditional brick and plate glass, with a saw-toothed roof of five gables. It is set into sloping but well drained ground, and therefore incorporates a basement as well as three storeys above ground. On its south-west face is a walled garden from which the building rises progressively in concrete terraces, each floor set back from the one below.

High thermal inertia principles have been employed in constructing the storage block (basement, ground and first floors), with thick ventilated and insulated cavity walls of concrete block. Those parts of the external walls of the storage area which are above ground have small, deeply recessed but unopenable windows. An air-handling system has been provided as an extra safeguard, with heating from a detached boiler on the far side of the garden. Piled foundations have enabled mobile racking to be used for all floors of storage, on an adjustable suspended floor.

Public and office areas employ glass to a greater extent than in any other British repository. Special glass has been used, incorporating a high degree of ultra-violet filtration. Its likely impact on the internal environment was the subject of a consultancy by Strathclyde university, and the results will be awaited with interest. Additional protection from sun-

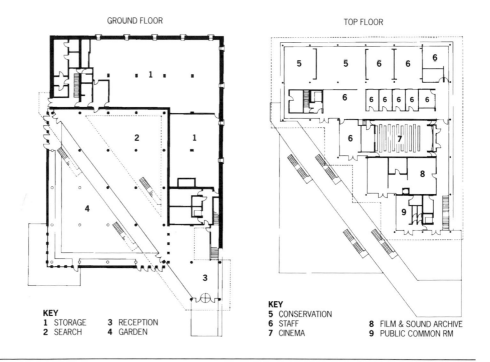

GROUND FLOOR

TOP FLOOR

KEY
1 STORAGE
2 SEARCH
3 RECEPTION
4 GARDEN

KEY
5 CONSERVATION
6 STAFF
7 CINEMA
8 FILM & SOUND ARCHIVE
9 PUBLIC COMMON RM

light is provided by blinds and by the overhang (at upper levels) of the roof and (at lower levels) of the concrete terracing.

The search room is on a classical triangular (3:4:5) ground-plan. The same proportions are reflected in the walled garden which it overlooks, and indeed in the roof line. The 'hypotenuse' wall, of almost uninterrupted glass with openable panels, is separated from the garden by a strip of water. Beside the window the area designated for consulting original records rises only one storey to its terrace roof, but at the rear towards the apex of the triangle, where microfilm and fiche are consulted, the room rises to the second level. There is seating for 30 readers of original documents plus 40 or more microfilm and fiche readers, and an area for maps and large documents (4 additional seats).

Other public facilities include (first floor) an education room with staircase access to the search room if required, and (third floor) a common room and a separate search room for the Wessex Film and Sound Archive (now brought into the record office for the first time), with an 85-seat cinema.

The main range of staff offices, some open-plan and some enclosed behind glazed partitions, and the generously large conservation workshop are also on the top floor, where the interior of the

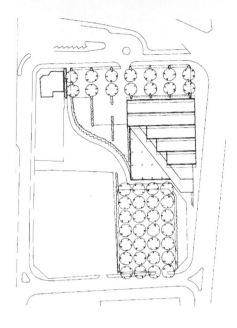

roof, carried on steel lattice, is exposed to view.

The storage space is expected to be sufficient for the next 25 years, and there is room for expansion on site.

Cost: approx. £5 million.

Storage (estimated): 13,000 linear metres.

Published reference:
'A new record office for the people of Hampshire' (Hampshire County Council booklet).

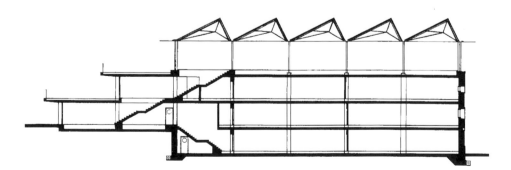

Hereford and Worcester Record Office

County Hall, Worcester
Hereford and Worcester County Council
Purpose-built, 1985

The County Council built this new repository, adjacent to County Hall on a green-field site about 2½ miles from the city centre, in 1985 to overcome storage problems in a number of other repositories and to provide liaison with a modern records management service centred in County Hall.

The building's external character – its brick facing and zinc-clad roof – owe much to the need to blend in with the existing buildings on the site, which it does with notable success. The slope of the land allows the public to enter on the upper of the building's two floors, whilst documents and staff have a separate entrance below. On each level the building is divided laterally, rather more than half being devoted to strong-rooms, one directly above the other. The remainder of the upper floor contains the public services and staff offices, whilst the lower floor houses document reception, reprographics studio and a plant room for the air-handling system. The boiler is housed in a detached building.

The windowless repository, with a 200mm internal shell of concrete block and 100mm cavity wall insulation, is partially air-conditioned (the air being heated, cooled and humidified as necessary, but not dehumidified or filtered). A separate room with an additional chiller unit has been designated a high security or special media strong room, and its metal racking specially earthed to reduce the risk to magnetic media from static electricity. Slight settlement in the upper floor has upset the smooth running of the mobile racking at that level.

The existing repository at St Helen's, Worcester was retained for storage and consultation of non-official records, and conservation services are provided from the office at Hereford (also extensively upgraded, in 1991), so the building here is smaller and more compact than would have been the case if it accommodated all the searchers or provided for all the functions of the combined service. It was designed to last for about 15 years, and

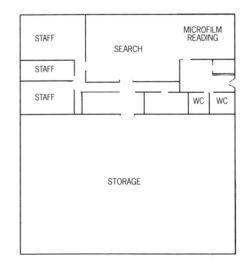

there is ample space for an extension over the present car park.

In the staff offices and public search rooms most of the walls are demountable partitions to allow for longer-term rearrangement of functions. The scheme did not provide any significant exhibition space nor a public meeting/ education room.

Cost: £625,317.

Storage: 1,285 square metres.

Published references:
Tony Wherry, 'Record office review: Worcester', in *Family Tree*, I no 5 (1985), p.18.
RW Cheney, 'Development of the county archive at Worcester', in Norton (IN-LOGOV 1986), pp.30–34.

Lancashire Record Office

Bow Lane, Preston
Lancashire County Council
Purpose–built storage block, 1988

A new record storage block for Lancashire Record Office was officially opened in 1988 on land adjacent to the record office (which was itself purpose-built in 1976, just before the period covered by this survey). This is one of the few British examples to date of modular extension to existing buildings. Another storage module is foreseen in the long term.

The ground-plan of the original building is a squared-off figure of eight, raised one storey off the ground on stilts from a podium, with a repository block rising as a solid core through one of the two 'quadrangles' in the design. The intention had been to allow expansion space in the second quadrangle by adding another storage block there, but that was ruled out on cost grounds, mainly owing to the difficulties in making the foundations sufficiently strong to carry the weight.

The new block, consisting of five storeys (with document reception and plant rooms at the lowest levels and four floors of storage above), is linked to the first by a glazed bridge at first-floor level. The block is of quite different design, an austere structure clad in dark brick, windowless save for the emergency stairwell at the rear. Internally, its steel frame is infilled with concrete blocks, which have been sealed and painted white to provide a bright working environment. The roof is clad in aluminium sheet.

The local climate and air quality dictated full air-conditioning with both filtration and washing in line with BS 5454 recommendations, and this is one of the very few repositories to have implemented the recommendations in full. Environmental conditions are strictly controlled and computer-monitored from the County Hall adjacent. In the aftermath of the

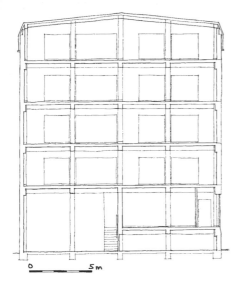

0   5m

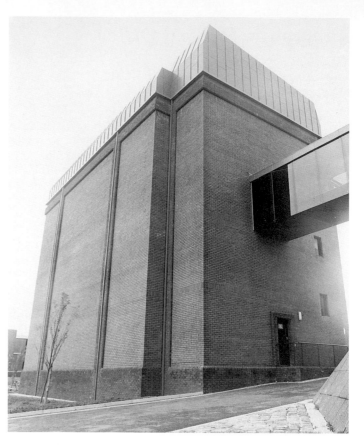

problems with air-conditioning at the PRO at Kew, which coincided with the planning phase of this building, the racking was designed with a generous clearance overhead, and the bases of the mobile systems were purpose-designed with large circular holes to promote air circulation. The only environmental problems experienced have been not strictly in this building at all, but in the linking bridge which has doors at both ends for security and as a result is poorly ventilated. The building is fitted throughout with smoke-detectors and intruder-alarms but has no automatic fire-extinction system, the brigade being only a few minutes away.

Installation of a lift in the new block provided the record office with a wel-come means of access for the disabled to the new building, which could previous-ly only be approached by a flight of stairs. External security is maintained by means of video-recording infra-red cameras and wall-mounted lights. The site is open-plan, with a small, tree-lined verge.

Storage: *c.* 1,600 sq. metres.

Lincolnshire Archives

St Rumbold Street, Lincoln
Lincolnshire County Council
Converted car showroom/factory, with purpose-built public block, 1991

Lincolnshire Archives moved in 1991 from the ancient administrative centre of the county, in Lincoln castle at the top of the hill, to a more commercial area at the bottom, about five minutes' walk from the railway station. Whereas Suffolk and Leicestershire, for example, converted existing buildings to house their public services and built on a new block for storage, here it was the other way round. A late Victorian (1897) brick-built bottling factory (subsequently turned into a car showroom), with a double pitched roof, provided the shell for the new repository, and on to this was built a new block to house the public services. A yard to the rear, protected by high railings, provides car parking space for both staff and public. The floors were stripped out of the old building and new piled foundations were driven, to bear the weight of mobile racking on two new levels of strongrooms carried on concrete floors, the upper one underpinned with steel. The storage space is divided into six windowless but air-conditioned compartments by new cavity walls of concrete block which enhance the overall thermal mass. Above the storage areas a top floor houses staff offices; a light, spacious and well equipped conservation workshop; and one of the most extensive reprographics operations in any British repository, with a photography studio and a suite of rooms for microfilming and for processing black and white and colour film, microfilm and microfiche. Surprisingly, given this particular specialism, no separate environmental provision has been made within the repository for the storage of new media. Among special features behind the scenes, the document reception area is subdivided into several work bays for staff, each equipped with benches and pigeonholes for sorting, and with a system of vacuum tubes for cleaning incoming records.

The public block, in red brick and prominently signed on the street frontage, also rests on piled foundations with a view to possible upward extension later. (Present capacity is estimated at 15 to 20 years). The attractively glazed entrance lobby opens into a reception area with display space, WCs and facilities for the deposit of coats and bags. The door into the search room is controlled by staff from behind a bank-style counter with louvred windows. The search room itself, apart from a number of carrels housing a reader-printer, ultra-violet lamp and facilities for typing or tape-recording, is a single open area. One long wall is occupied by microfilm readers, and the remainder of the generous space is available for consultation of original records, including maps and outsize documents. Upstairs, a lecture room/education room accommodates up to 100, and has separate WC facilities.

Cost: £2 million.

Storage: 13,000 sq ft.

Published references:
C Johnson and S Noble, 'New premises', in *Society of Archivists Newsletter*, 60 (March 1992), p.17.

C Johnson. *A hive of industry. An account of the St Rumbold Street area of Lincoln* (Lincoln 1992).

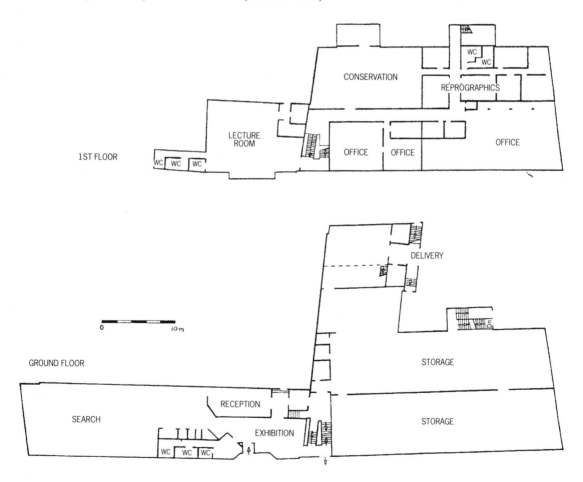

Museum of Science and Industry in Manchester

Liverpool Road Station, Manchester
Independent charitable trust with grant-in-aid from the Department of National Heritage
Converted basement of a Victorian warehouse, 1988

The museum was established on the Liverpool Road Station site in 1983. In 1988 development of the Lower Byrom Street warehouse on the site offered an opportunity to establish a purpose-built repository for the museum's archives (Building Design Partnership). This was built in the basement, accommodating three strongrooms and a public area comprising library/search room and offices, together with a reception area/exhibition space. Air-conditioning for the strongrooms and searchroom was provided by adjacent plant, linked to other facilities in the building. A lift was installed to provide access from other floors of the warehouse.

In order to minimise the risks from damp and flooding in the basement, the storage area was built on a platform raised artificially above the original floor level and detached from the exterior walls, allowing it to be surrounded by drainage and service channels. As an additional security measure flood–alarms were installed.

Liverpool Road Station is the oldest surviving passenger railway station in the world. Both the station and its adjacent warehouses are therefore of special historical interest. In order to preserve the character of the warehouse (a listed building), its ceiling of cast iron beams and brick jack arches was left exposed instead of being hidden behind an artificial ceiling. In order to inhibit damaging flaking, the brickwork was treated with a clear sealant. Large cast iron and brick pillars supporting the upper floors necessitated careful planning of the layout of racking, but the challenge was well met by a mixture of mobile and static racking, with horizontal plan chests, and vertical storage for pictures. New internal walls are of breeze block.

As the Record Centre is entirely accommodated below ground there is no natural light. But a light and spacious working environment for staff and visitors has been achieved using glazed panels rather than opaque walls to separate the search room from the offices and reception area. Reproductions of images from the collections are on display in the reception area, to welcome visitors and to indicate the Centre's scope.

A new object store has been built in the basement adjoining the archive, and the museum plans in future to convert the whole basement into an 'access and resource area'. This will link the stored collections of objects and archives, and provide a searchroom and on-line database for access to the collections and information. It will be linked by a ramp and lifts to the main reception and circulation areas of the museum.

The museum received a 50% capital grant of £120,000 from the Office of Arts and Libraries towards the building. Further grants towards shelving materials have been received from the North West Museums Service, to allow progressive upgrading of storage conditions.

Cost: £240,000 (1988).

Storage: approx. 950 sq metres.

Published reference:
Stella Butler and Ann Jones, 'The Greater Manchester Museum of Science and Industry library and reference centre', in *Proceedings of the Business Archives Council Annual Conference 1989*.

[unpubl.] Ann Jones, 'Accommodating an archive' – paper presented to an AIM seminar, December 1990.

National Film Archive:
J Paul Getty Jr Conservation Centre

Kingshill House, Berkhamsted
British Film Institute
Purpose–built, 1986/87

On a green-field site on a hillside above Berkhamsted, the principal repository for the National Film Archive's safety film and video collection is built in the grounds of the historic Kingshill House, which has now been converted into offices.

The Centre, sponsored by J Paul Getty Jr, KBE (architects: Nickolls King Design), provides state-of-the-art storage repositories respectively for (1) acetate and polyester-based film and video, (2) cellulose nitrate film awaiting copying and conservation (the main nitrate store being at Gaydon, Warwickshire), (3) colour master material, and (4) posters, stills and paper-based archives, in an inter-linked complex of buildings clad in red brick and radiating from a central reception block, set in a pleasantly landscaped concourse.

Considerable attention has been paid to the specification of the air-conditioning and environmental controls, and the plant has already been upgraded in line with the latest scientific advice on the

preservation of the respective media. The current parameters set are 18°C and 35%RH for acetate; 18°C and 50%RH

for paper (but 13°C and 55% RH in a new paper store under construction), 18°C and 50% RH for nitrate, and 6°C and 35–40% RH for colour master material. The air is filtered to remove potentially harmful particulates, and the low relative humidity is maintained (where required) by machinery employing desiccant salts.

The acetate stores are enclosed within double brick walls, the cavity insulated with bonded polystyrene beads. The roof comprises 100mm of rigid foam with an aluminium skin, topped with steel. The reinforced concrete floors required precision engineering both to take the great load of static metal racking reaching to a height of some 20 feet, and to allow the smooth passage of the mobile elevator trucks that have to be manouevred down the aisles to fetch and replace the film. Some natural daylight is provided through large double-glazed but unopenable windows, and the electric lighting is controlled by means of passive infra-red sensors. Smoke-detectors throughout the building are linked to the fire brigade.

The paper stores are additionally protected by a halon automatic fire-extinction system.

A feature probably unique in the United Kingdom is the store for cellulose nitrate film, cast in a single concrete mould, divided into 24 small cells with steel doors to limit the risk from this potentially self-igniting medium, with an anti-blast wall down the spinal corridor and 6,000 gallons of water standing ready to flood the roof in the event of an emergency. There are many additional precautions: for example all the electrical cabling and fittings have been designed to be spark-proof.

The site also includes laboratories and offices, but no public research or viewing facilities. Expansion space is available for additional stores.

Storage: acetate 3 × 5,250 cubic metres; nitrate 24 × 4.8 cubic metres; paper 3 × 720 cubic metres, plus 2 × 810 cubic metres under construction.

National Library of Wales

Aberystwyth
Purpose-built Manuscripts reading room, 1986

The accommodation of the Department of Manuscripts at the National Library of Wales has been adapted and extended in several phases during the period under review, and further changes are under consideration. The new reading room was perhaps the most important single development, in that it gave the Department for the first time its own public areas, clearly demarcated from the Library's other public facilities.

To achieve this a new two-storey structure was created within one of the courtyards of the original building, adjacent to much of the Department's existing storage space. The outer walls of the original building, overlooking the courtyard, were retained as the shell of the new structure, and a free-standing inner wall was constructed of concrete block, leaving an inspection and insulation cavity in between. The lower storey (ground level) houses an air-conditioned strongroom fitted with mobile racking, and the upper a suite of public and staff rooms. At the upper level the solid shell of the original building was pierced at three points to give access to the new building. Public entry is by way of the main library corridor and through one of these new doors into, first, a catalogue and reference room housing card indexes, the Library's own reference catalogues and some related reference works. Behind the staff counter (appropriately shaped like a question-mark) is the library assistants' room with its own direct link, through the second of the new doors, into the storage areas. Also at the rear of the catalogue room, a small area was intended to serve for microfilm readers but quickly proved inadequate for the growing demand: microfilm holdings are therefore now consulted in a specially adapted part of the Library's main read-

ing room. A glazed partition next to the reference counter overlooks the manuscripts reading room.

The reading room, rectangular, with a single central pillar, is arranged with three long rows of tables each accommodating 10 readers. Another glazed partition separates this from the superintendent's room, allowing good sight-lines for invigilation. Natural light is provided both here and on a smaller scale in the other rooms through multi-faceted pyramid roof lights of frosted glass, which have not however proved entirely leak-proof and have (in extreme external weather conditions) occasionally suffered from condensation. In the centre of the reading room a grid of square baffles deflects any direct sunlight away from manuscripts. The walls, panelled in light wood, are fitted with bookshelves housing finding aids for other Welsh, British and overseas repositories, and printed reference works. A further new door gives access to the Library's main reading room beyond.

The overall effect is comfortable and conducive to quiet study, apart from the noise of the air-conditioning system (which is the only means of air supply to this otherwise enclosed area), which some readers find distracting.

Cost of reading room: £745,000.

Published reference:
D Huws, 'The National Library of Wales: a building and its adaptation', in Dewe pp.88–101.

Northamptonshire Record Office

Wootton Hall Park, Northampton
Northamptonshire County Council
Purpose-built, 1991

There could scarcely be a greater contrast than that between the cramped and inconvenient quarters of Northamptonshire Record Office's former historic home at Delapre Abbey which had served it since 1957, and the new building begun in 1989 as part of the County Council's commemoration of its centenary. The latter is designed not only to meet as nearly as possible the needs of today's record office and its users, but also to last for at least another century. For budgetary reasons the whole enterprise had to be undertaken with remarkable speed, and its undoubted overall success is a tribute to the skills and team-work of the county archivist and the architect.

Some of the inspiration came from West Sussex Record Office, much of whose brief proved readily adaptable to the particular work-flow of Northants, and some from the Suffolk Record Office at Ipswich which supplied computerised data on its own experiment with high thermal inertia. The design, however, is different from either of these models.

Situated on a 1.8 acre green-field site some three miles from the city centre, but well served by buses and with ample car parking space, the record office is on a campus adjacent to the police and fire headquarters. This not only offers peace of mind, but also does away with the need to have automatic fire extinction (though the building is protected by smoke/heat detectors which alert the brigade directly). It consists of three linked blocks housing respectively the repository (two storeys), and the public services and administration (each one storey).

The internal frame of the staff offices and public block is of galvanised steel, with walls of red brick. The repository block is of heavyweight masonry and concrete construction, its external walls of brickwork and blockwork 655mm thick, with concrete columns, floors and inner roof. All three blocks have sweeping, red-tiled roofs which overhang substantially, to shade and protect the walls below. Building materials have been selected for durability and minimal maintenance.

The windowless repository is built over a basement which houses the county's emergency planning headquarters, an arrangement believed to be unique in the country. The weight of the troughed concrete ceilings/floors in this block is supported on concrete columns and beams, and on the external walls. Environmental stability is maintained substantially without mechanical intervention, by thick insulated double cavity walls. With portable dehumidifiers to assist during the building's drying out, stable temperature and relative humidity were attained almost from the start. The mobile racking within the repository rests on a suspended floor which can be adjusted to maintain absolute horizontality should there be deflection in the main structure.

The large rectangular public areas are uninterrupted by columns, and although the functions (reception, catalogues, search) are clearly defined and segregated, all are spacious and well appointed. There are seats for 50 readers of archives and 18 of microforms. The rooms designated for the Northamptonshire Record Society's library and for education/group visits are separated from each other and from the reception area by sliding wooden partitions which can be opened up to create a large circulation- or meeting space when required.

The meticulous attention to often overlooked details of furnishings, fixtures and fittings deserves special mention. To take just a few examples, windows in the two smaller blocks are openable at the top, to prevent papers blowing about, but background ventilation can also be adjusted

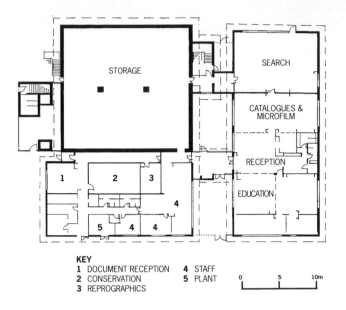

KEY
1 DOCUMENT RECEPTION 4 STAFF
2 CONSERVATION 5 PLANT
3 REPROGRAPHICS

0   5   10m

by means of shallow, tilting grilles at the foot of each window. Furniture has been chosen to be interchangeable virtually throughout the office. A public telephone in the reception area has been sited at a height that is easily reached from a wheel chair. Lockers purpose-designed to hold a coat and a bag have proved so popular that readers have even been known to leave their possessions there uncollected during a fire alarm test.

Curiously, there is no covered delivery bay for the reception of records, and the staff accommodation and general storage space were victims of a tight budget and are by no means generous. But this must still be rated one of the most impressive and successful buildings of the present generation.

Cost: £2 million (excl. site), plus £400,000 for furnishing.

Storage: 2 × 466 square metres.

Published reference:
'Guardians into the next century', in *County Councils Gazette*, June 1991.

North Devon Record Office

Tuly Street, Barnstaple
Devon County Council
Purpose-built within library, 1988

Barnstaple is 40 miles by road from the headquarters of the Devon Record Office in Exeter. Plans had long been laid for a branch record office here, to be located in a new branch library. An historic, town-centre site beside the castle mound was purchased as early as 1973 (when it was encumbered with the remains of a mineral water factory). But it was 1984 before funds became available for building to

proceed. The factory was demolished and an archaeological investigation undertaken.

The sensitive nature and location of the site imposed constraints on the height, shape and character of the building. It was limited to four storeys, the steel and concrete structure being clad with red brick and colonnaded on three sides, in order to 'reflect dignity, simplicity and a feeling of belonging to Barnstaple: a building of solidity but with some light relief, restrained but modern'.

One of the aims was to pool the local studies resources of the county library and county record office with those of the North Devon Athenaeum, comfortably the senior partner in the venture and celebrating its centenary in the year the new building opened. For maximum convenience to staff and users the three services preferably had to be accommodated on the same floor, and this was eventually achieved, on the second floor, after careful juggling with space. The same floor also houses the Henry Williamson room, a meeting room for up to 60 people.

The archive strongroom is air-conditioned to BS 5454 standard, perhaps especially desirable in a westerly maritime climate, but it also has openable windows fitted with ultra-violet filters and blinds. The archives reading room, seating 11 plus a further 6 microfilm readers, is separated from the library by a row of bookshelves. Among the few drawbacks of an otherwise successful scheme, staff accommodation is awkwardly sited in the centre, at one remove from natural light, although with full-length windows on to the central passage and the public rooms beyond. There is no space for either lateral or vertical expansion once the present storage is filled, although the strongroom has not yet been racked to its full capacity.

Conservation, reprographics and management services are provided at the County Record Office in Exeter.

Cost: not separately costed; part of a larger project.

Storage: 700 linear metres.

Published references:
Harrison (1990) pp.127–129. L Rose and M Rowe, 'The new North Devon Record Office', in *Archives*, XIX no 85 (April 1991), pp.289–296; *New Library News* No 6, (Devon County Council, Barnstaple, Sept 1987); 'North Devon Area Library and Record Office, Barnstaple' (Devon CC leaflet).

North Yorkshire County Record Office

Northallerton
North Yorkshire County Council
Converted furniture warehouse/factory, 1991

The rather bleak exterior of much of this single storey building, two minutes' walk from County Hall and the railway station, does little to prepare the visitor for the spacious and well appointed interior. Here are brought together, for the first time under one roof, all the records in the County Council's care which were previously scattered in 'several warrens of small and inefficient rooms' in Northallerton and Ripon, including county hall itself, law courts, prison cells, store rooms and a poor-law institution. The total area of 28,000 sq ft is only about 8% larger than the combined area of those premises, but this time it is a carefully planned unity, laid out and racked to give far more efficient and cost-effective use of space to meet all present requirements and provide for several decades more, and generally to improve upon the working conditions of staff and public alike, with enhanced amenities.

Much of the original building was clad with insulated corrugated steel, but with a solid concrete wall along part of the south side. Except in that part, new concrete-block walls were built within the shell to provide greater security and

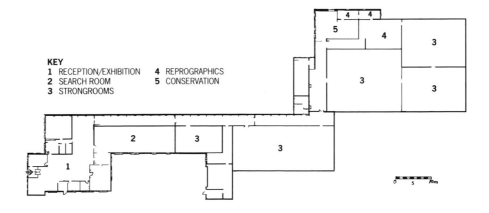

KEY
1 RECEPTION/EXHIBITION   **4** REPROGRAPHICS
2 SEARCH ROOM   **5** CONSERVATION
3 STRONGROOMS

assist environmental control. Compartments have been constructed within the originally open-plan warehouse to provide five strongrooms, windowless and partially air-conditioned. There is a substantial further storage area which could be converted in the longer term. In order to make best use of a long, narrow site, and incidentally to reduce to an absolute minimum the quantity of external wall abutting the strongrooms, a service corridor has been created immediately inside the south wall of the building, linking staff offices and public areas, conveniently set apart at the front of the building, with the storage areas and technical work areas at the rear, protected by a series of security/fire doors along the corridor.

The project ranks among the cheapest covered by this volume. Further expenditure will, however, be necessary at an early date to improve the roof and provide additional racking to make best use of the space, so the final bill remains to be reckoned. Even so, it seems likely to represent good value for money overall.

The front door opens on to a generously large, carpeted reception area, with space for exhibitions and display of publications. This hub gives access to all the public facilities and senior staff offices. The search room, which on account of a rigorous local policy to keep wear and tear on original documents to a minimum and improve retrieval time is mainly for consultation of microfilm copies, is equipped with a score of 16 and 35mm microfilm readers. Its generous space compared with the old county hall searchroom means that visitors now rarely have to be turned away. The extent of the frustration this must have been causing was demonstrated by an immediate surge in the number of users on the opening of the new building, which if it continues will soon put pressure even on this enhanced search capacity. A small tea room in which readers can eat their sandwiches is an additional facility.

The site has also provided ample space for a microfilm and reprographics suite, conservation laboratory and staff common room.

Cost: £325,000 (purchase of site); plus £355,000 (conversion and fitting out).

Nottinghamshire Archives

Nottingham
Nottinghamshire County Council
Purpose-built, 1992 to open 1993

From four buildings and 50 storage rooms to a single two-storey building with two storage areas: such was the eagerly anticipated move awaiting Nottinghamshire Archives when the new building, completed but not yet occupied, was inspected for this survey. Situated beside a canal (though well above water level), and only two minutes' walk from the railway station, at the corner of a site shortly to be developed for new magistrates' courts, the record office is conveniently located in a pleasantly landscaped precinct with its own small car park, and shielded by a high brick wall from a busy main road.

The frame is of steel, the floors of reinforced concrete, and the walls of brick, faced externally in three colours: red, blue and buff. The generously overhanging roof is tiled in artificial slate, with an insulated cavity below. The storage area is air-conditioned and the whole building protected by smoke- and intruder-detectors.

The design, in two storeys throughout, expresses a simple but effective segregation of functions. A large square block houses public areas and staff offices. At the opposite end of the site a still larger rectangular block houses the records. In between a smaller square block links the two, with an economical spinal corridor off which are the technical and plant facilities (a reprographics workshop and power switches on the ground floor, and the conservation workshop and plant room upstairs).

The main public area, on the ground floor, is largely open-plan, with a central invigilation and enquiry desk for staff overseeing four study areas for catalogues, original records (18 seats), microforms (30 seats) and library materials, demarcated by low-level shelving and furniture. Locker facilities, WCs and a small refreshment room for the public are located immediately inside the main entrance. The foyer also gives controlled access to a small lecture/meeting room for up to 30 people on the first floor, with separate WC facilities so that this area can function as a self-contained unit.

The strongrooms are equipped predominantly with new steel shelving, mobile on the ground floor and static above. The

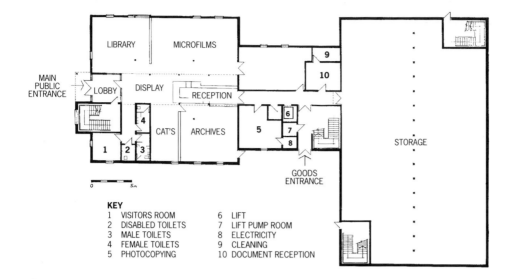

KEY
1 VISITORS ROOM
2 DISABLED TOILETS
3 MALE TOILETS
4 FEMALE TOILETS
5 PHOTOCOPYING
6 LIFT
7 LIFT PUMP ROOM
8 ELECTRICITY
9 CLEANING
10 DOCUMENT RECEPTION

rooms are windowless, despite outward appearances where dummy windows have been fitted in symmetry with the real ones required on the internal fire-escape stairs.

Staff offices are mainly grouped around a central open-plan work room, and additional amenities include a staff room and shower. The conservation workshop, long and rectangular, has plenty of direct north light and a view over the canal. Special attention has been paid throughout the building to the ducting for power, computer, and voice, both through under-floor cabling in the public areas, and continuous circuitry at dado level in the staff offices.

Cost: approx. £2 million excluding land.

Storage: (est.) 7,674 linear metres.

Post Office Archives

Mount Pleasant, London EC
Conversion of former boiler house, Mount Pleasant HQ, 1992

Although the Post Office left the civil service in 1969 its records (dating from the 17th century) are designated public by the Public Records Act 1958. Their storage accommodation accordingly has to be approved by the Lord Chancellor. In this case the building was actually opened, inspected, (and indeed blessed) by the Lord Chancellor himself, Lord Mackay, in March 1992.

It occupies the site of the former boiler house of the Mount Pleasant sorting office, splendidly converted into a two-storey structure of brick, glass and steel, housing search room and offices in two separate sections of the ground floor, and strong room and plant room in the basement, served by a passenger lift.

Special thought has been given to access by the disabled. Glazed sliding front doors give access to an entrance lobby with a mat inscribed with words of welcome. The door from this reception area into the search room is controlled by staff from the other side of a security window.

The search room, air-conditioned and comfortably furnished in pastel shades, is hung with posters and paintings from the Post Office collection. It incorporates within one large open-plan area not only (i) study tables (with under floor cabling to allow for use of lap-top computers), but also (ii) open access to a reference library including postal history journals, and also to some of the most used genealogical sources, and (iii) a rest area with a drinks vending machine. This particular integration of functions raises a number of environmental questions and cannot be recommended for wide adoption, but in the context of this small search room catering for a dozen readers plus three microfilm readers – with good sight-lines for invigilation supplemented by closed circuit TV surveillance – it works well enough.

The single strongroom, an impressively large windowless area in the basement, is also air-conditioned, with temperature and RH controlled in line with BS 5454.

Its tall (Apex) mobile racking has greatly improved the utilisation of space compared with the previous premises in Southwark. The lighting in the aisles, which is attached by brackets to the top of the mobile systems and moves with them, can be controlled on time switches to reduce unnecessary energy consumption. Automatic smoke detectors have been installed, and the brigade is immediately to hand. The security system is linked to the main sorting office building, and out of hours the entire ground floor street frontage is protected by lockable steel roller blinds (*see illustration on p.31*).

Cost: £1¼ million.

Storage: approx. 5,000 linear metres.

Published reference:
Leaflet, 'The Post Office Archives'.

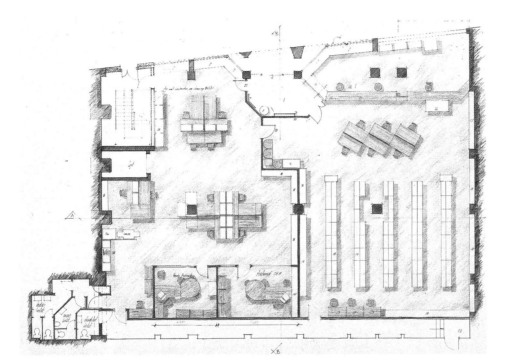

Public Record Office

Kew
Purpose-built, 1977

By the mid 1960s, storage space for records in the original, purpose-built Victorian repository of the Public Record Office at Chancery Lane was already in short supply, and even with maximum use of its large out-store in a former military hospital at Ashridge, Herts, additional space was urgently required. The option of extending Sir James Pennethorne's building was explored but rapidly dismissed as an inadequate solution to the long-term storage problem. But at the same time it was thought too valuable to abandon, and the Office chose instead to build a second major repository, when offered a Crown-owned site beside the Thames at Kew, inconveniently distant from central London.

An outline brief was prepared in 1969, but the plans were modified by Richmond Borough Council in 1971 reducing the height from 28 to 22 metres to make a less forceful impact on the skyline. It was 1973 before the contract was let, and the building did not open to the public until 1977. It was being designed (for the Property Services Agency) as BS 5454 was in preparation, and was the first repository built with the Standard's recommendations specifically in mind.

This is by far the largest archive repository in the country, occupying seven floors (two below ground) with a net area of 33,440 square metres. The building, a vast square structure carried on a reinforced concrete frame on pile-driven

foundations, with internal concrete pillars on a 9.6 metre square grid, is faced with pre-stressed concrete panels and glass. Staff offices and a number of services such as catering, security and reprographics occupy the ground floor (4,760 sq. metres gross); public searchrooms, reference room, library, computer rooms, conservation and more staff offices the first floor (6,102 sq. metres). The upper three floors (7,140 sq. metres each), cantilevered out beyond the lower floors, are largely given over to archive storage. The basement, originally also intended for this purpose, has not been used for archives because of the (slight but inescapable) risk of flooding, both from the river and from the many water services which traverse the ceiling. The sub-basement, tanked with a 1.5 metres thick concrete floor, is a plant room on a scale worthy of an ocean liner or a township, with its own electricity substation, emphasising how power-intensive this building is. There is a double roof, the inner level a concrete slab topped with pre-felted expanded polystyrene, fibre insulation board and two layers of bitumen felt; a void; and then a stainless steel outer roof (supported on a timber frame), designed not only to offer further protection against the rain but also to reflect sunlight and minimise solar gain.

From the start, it has been something of a showpiece, influential in inspiring many British and foreign archivists to raise their sights. It is impressively endowed with what, even a generation on, still seems to many like technological wizardry: a computer-controlled requisitioning system, reader-paging, a continuous 'paternoster' elevator for transporting records between floors, and electric, driver-operated trolleys for delivering records from the shelves to the paternoster. At its best, with this mechanical assistance, it promised very fast production times for records ordered in the search room. But technology, as well as its human masters, can be temperamental.

The public areas are comfortably furnished and, thanks to careful planning of the acoustics, reasonably impervious to the inevitable bustle of a national archives. And it is perhaps these areas have have proved most consistently successful. There is a feeling of spaciousness, from the large open foyer area, (now developed to incorporate locker space, a sales point for publications and an intro-

ductory video, as well as the public restaurant) through the landing with its wall-mounted exhibition cases, into the reference room, deliberately segregated from the search rooms for consultation of finding aids and reference books and requisitioning of records, and finally into the main search room. Fixtures and fittings have worn well, especially the purpose-designed light oak search room tables and reference desks with light green leather tops.

The original plan incorporated an overflow search room of equal size, but projections of reader visits proved excessive. This is just as well, because the space has been needed for other uses: conveniently partitioned to provide staff offices, a room for group visits and a self-service microfilm reading room.

These are not the only adaptations to have been made to the original layout. The Office's changing administrative structure and its diversification into new areas, particularly information technology including preparation for the receipt of machine-readable archives, have been among the factors requiring new partitioning. In the case of the computer suite this has required the construction of a self-contained room with its own air-conditioning units within the area originally designed for the staff library.

In this respect the large, square and basically open-plan floors have served the Office's changing accommodation requirements of the past fifteen years surprisingly well. But the enormous area and volume of each floor, the basic square shape and the decision to sandwich the public areas between storage and office accommodation have all in their own way produced problems. The short-comings of the air-conditioning

system are separately discussed [see p.50]. Daylight scarcely penetrates to the centre of the square. This is deliberate in the storage areas, but less happy in the offices and work spaces, some of which have to rely entirely on artificial light. The experiment with open-plan offices on the ground floor has not been a success, the senior staff in particular finding the levels of noise and distraction stressful where partitions are thin and stop short of the ceiling in order not to impede the air flow.

The building is fitted throughout with smoke-detectors. Surprisingly, given the status of the records, but understandably, given the size and cost of the plant which would have been necessary, it has no automatic fire-extinction system. But it is well provided with ionisation smoke detectors, hand-held extinguishers and hose reels. Each of the storage floors is partially compartmented into units of 2,500 sq. metres with fire doors which close automatically in the event of an alarm. It is manned and patrolled 24 hours a day.

Cost: £8 million.

Storage: 100,000 linear metres.

Published references:
Bell, L. 'The new Public Record Office at Kew', in *JSA*, 5 no 1 (April 1974), pp.1–7.
Cox, N. 'The new Public Record Office at Kew', in *Archivum*, 31 (1986), pp.133–142.
'The new building at Kew', in *19th Report of the Keeper of Public Records* (1977), pp.25–28.
Miller, G. 'Public Records Office Kew', in *Construction*, 25 (1978), pp.11–13.
Bashforth, P. 'Public Record Office Kew', in *Construction* 26 (1978), pp.5–8.

Sheffield Archives

Shoreham Street, Sheffield
Sheffield City Council
Converted car showroom, 1989

Sheffield Archives is unusual in having a river flowing beneath it (actually an old friend, as it also flowed beneath the previous premises in Ellin Street). It is admittedly a small river and is culverted, nor does it flow beneath the storage areas, but its very existence called for careful appraisal to ensure that there was no risk of flooding before the conversion of the former Autoways car showroom as an archives could be seriously considered. In other respects, and particularly on account of its solid flooring, this made a natural choice.

Outwardly an inconspicuous two-storey semi-industrial building situated on a busy main road, and not central despite being only a few minutes' walk from the railway station, it has been divided into two holdings, one for the archives office

and the other for a number of audio-visual companies whose concern with records of another kind was a factor in the re-naming of the Archives (formerly known as Sheffield Record Office).

The planning of the project was carried out by two successive principal archivists, two architects and two directors of libraries. But although this discontinuity caused its own difficulties, the main problems and constraints were generated by other factors such as the necessity to divide the building into two separate units because the whole was too large for the Archives' needs, and the tightly cash-limited budget available for the project, which among other things led to the abandonment of early plans to include accommodation here for the conservation service (which in the event remained in the premises of the former South Yorkshire County Record Office in Ellin Street and under separate management).

The shared tenancy has worked reasonably well, although it demanded special security and fire precautions for the benefit of both parties. The other tenants were assigned space immediately above the archive storage area, whose ceiling therefore had to be tanked against the risk of water penetration in the event of fire-fighting in the premises above. The most convenient division of the building left the only lift technically outside the archives office in a shared loading bay. For the most part it is more convenient for records required for staff or educational use on the first floor to be carried up the stairs, although the lift is used for heavier loads, and also to assist disabled access to the education room.

The long, double-glazed street frontage on the ground floor, screened against ultra-violet light and fitted with vertical slatted blinds to reduce glare, insulates the public reception area and searchroom from the worst of the noise and distraction of the street, although not from all the dust. Despite a somewhat angular ground plan, the search room affords a pleasant and comfortable working area with space for up to 24 readers. A further-

er, windowless room accommodates 13 microfilm readers.

Two air-conditioned strongrooms have been provided, the main one a large single area fitted with a mixture of static and mobile racking and, at this early date, still having ample free space for additional racking in future. The smaller room, for special (mainly audio-visual) media, has separate environmental controls. Both are protected by smoke detectors and an automatic halon fire-extinction system. Apart from the almost predictable teething troubles with the air-conditioning equipment, which at its best has proved well capable of maintaining a stable environment, the main difficulty has been over the level of lighting in the large strongroom, where calculations of the lighting necessary for a given area, although made in accordance with BS 5454, did not take account of the substantial presence of high mobile racking. This has now been solved.

The first floor holds staff offices and common room and an education room large enough to accommodate a class of 30 in comfort.

Cost: £700,000.

Storage: 21,000 linear ft.

Southampton University Library

Archives and special collections
Purpose-built, 1987

In 1982 the papers of the first Duke of Wellington, accepted for the nation in lieu of tax, were provisionally allocated by the Minister for the Arts to Southampton University on condition that they were housed in secure conditions and a controlled environment.

A group of rooms in the university library was specially adapted during 1982/83 to provide a strongroom, search room, conservation laboratory and staff offices, at a cost of around £50,000 which was substantially met by donations from a number of private trusts and individuals. The university's archival and manuscript holdings continued to increase rapidly in the years immediately following. This gave added urgency to the more general provision of increased library accommodation under the University Grants Committee's capital works programme between 1985 and 1987. The new, purpose-built archive department (architects Gutteridge

Woodford Chambers), situated on the top floor of a three-storey brick extension, comprises lobby, public searchroom for 16 readers, and strongroom. In the same development a twin strongroom, initially for book collections, is due to be developed for archival use in 1993.

The exterior brickwork (builders Brazier and Sons Ltd) was the southern regional winner of the Quality Brickwork Award 1990 made by the Brick Development Association and *Building Magazine*. Internally, on the recommendation of the National Museums Security Adviser, particular attention has been paid to security, making this one of the most thoroughly protected repositories in the whole of the United Kingdom. Several different kinds of intruder detectors are employed at strategic points, with a panic button for staff use in an emergency. The archives department is effectively isolated from the rest of the library

behind locked doors which admit the reader first into a self-contained lobby separated from the reading room by a further locked door. Invigilation is assisted by closed-circuit television.

The strongroom is air-conditioned throughout the 24 hours by a computer-controlled system, and is protected in the event of fire by an automatic halon 1301 fire-extinction system.

The rooms adapted in the earlier phase of development have been further adapted, with the former reading room now pro-viding work space shared flexibly by curatorial and conservation staff, who have benefited from working closely together.

Cost: Part of a wider development, not separately costed.

Storage: 186.8 sq. metres before 1993 development.

Published reference:
Harrison 1990, pp.37–39.

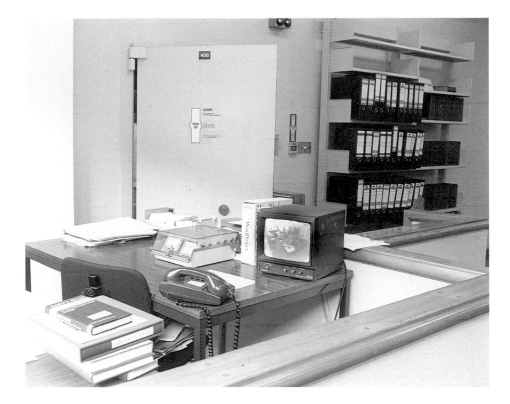

Suffolk Record Office

Gatacre Road, Ipswich
Suffolk County Council
Converted school, with purpose-built repository, 1990

By the mid 1980s the archives held by the Ipswich branch of Suffolk Record Office had spilled over into more than 30 store rooms. The opportunity arose in 1987 to acquire a handsome, single-storey Victorian board school (1888) in Bramford Road, to house the public services of a new record office, and to add a purpose-built two-storey repository and office block in the former playground. The site is remote from the town centre but on a bus route. It was used latterly as a drama centre (and a regional theatre company still occupies a small part of it). The planning authority insisted that the height of the repository should not exceed that of the school buildings, and a number of other problems were posed by the site: deep trench foundations were required, to carry the building on soft terrain; excess water had to be separately drained away without using the adjacent street drains, and a special electricity sub-station had to be built.

The repository, whose weight is borne on concrete columns and a reinforced concrete slab, has a double cavity wall faced in red brick in keeping with the original Victorian buildings, and is linked to them by a new glazed corridor which borders a pleasant landscaped garden. This still leaves ample space for a car park and for possible future expansion. The new building was officially opened by the Princess of Wales in February 1990, and later that year won one of the awards of the Ipswich Society to owners, developers and builders whose work was felt to have improved the town.

Although most of the public services are concentrated in the older building, the entrance is not through one of the school doors but through a new glass portico into the corridor linking the two buildings. This sets a lively modern tone for the new venture, which is continued in the old building by the use of bright colours. The original high-pitched ceilings of the schoolrooms and halls have been retained, giving an open and proudly lofty feel to the reception room,

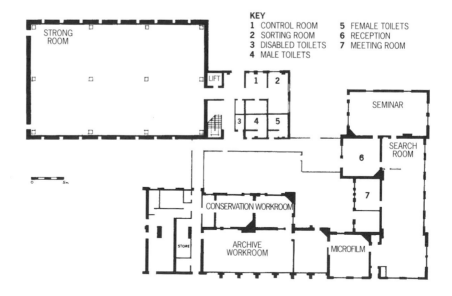

KEY

1 CONTROL ROOM   5 FEMALE TOILETS
2 SORTING ROOM   6 RECEPTION
3 DISABLED TOILETS   7 MEETING ROOM
4 MALE TOILETS

education room and search room (20 seats), where fireplaces and other original details have been nicely preserved. Uplighting on to a white ceiling effectively meets the needs of the search room, where the overall effect is both spacious and restful, but the decisions to retain the polished wooden floors (rather than introduce carpeting), and the original single glazing (despite constant noise from the adjacent main road) may need early review. Further former classrooms have adapted well to microform reading room (20 seats) and staff offices, but more extensive structural alteration was required to make a suitably spacious conservation workshop out of three former rooms.

The repository block, isolated from the public areas by electronic security locks operable only by the staff, was the first in the United Kingdom designed on European models to achieve high thermal inertia. It is described in more detail on p.21. It has proved remarkably successful in its main objective of providing stable environmental conditions at low cost without the need for air conditioning. Among its other features the tall but narrow and deeply recessed, openable windows were designed to admit some natural light, and may be used to assist in environmental control. They also soften the visual impact, both internally and externally, where there would otherwise have been a solid wall. The generously overhanging roof, supported on brightly coloured steel girders, protects the walls from damp and heat. Fire- and intruder-detectors and alarms are fitted, but there is no automatic fire-extinction system, the brigade being only a few minutes away. One drawback is that there are no satisfactory catering facilities in the neighbourhood.

Cost: £1.8 million.

Storage: 21,690 linear ft.

Published references:
Jones; Newsletter of the Suffolk Record Office 3 (Oct 1990); Society of Archivists Newsletter 54 pp.11–12.

West Sussex Record Office

Orchard Street, Chichester
West Sussex County Council
Purpose-built, 1989

From its foundation in 1946 West Sussex Record Office occupied converted premises, successively in the basement of county hall (1946–68) and then in a William and Mary town house in West Street specially restored for the purpose (1968–89). By the late 1970s the structure of the latter building was deteriorating, and its storage accommodation was overflowing. The nature of the building presented other constraints to a growing public

service. Public and staff areas could not be fully segregated, technical and cloakroom facilities were inadequate and there was no provision for access by the disabled. After protracted negotiations the site for a new record office was found on a former council car park nearby.

The nature of the site required deep piled foundations, on which was erected a two-storey building, steel and concrete-framed with a brick facing. Considerable care was taken in the choice of materials so that they would be fully in sympathy with their brick and flint surroundings. Attention to details in the exterior, such as the styling of the small tower required for the cooling plant and the contouring of tiles on what might have been an austere solid wall facing adjacent housing, has helped present a human face to the outside world.

The design is a classic statement of the physical separation of five distinct functions: public areas, staff offices, document reception, repository and plant. The principal repository areas, windowless, comprise four strongrooms of equal size (27 × 11 metres), two on each floor. The plan to use two distinct floors in the repository was adopted in order to give maximum floor-loading capacity throughout and to assist in environmental control. On three sides the strongrooms are surrounded by other functions, leaving only one external, south-facing wall. This helps maintain environmental stability and conserve energy, and although the repository is fitted with full air conditioning it has not been found necessary to keep the system running twenty-four hours a day.

Public access is controlled from a spacious reception area with provision for

publicity and small displays. The single L-shaped search room, with seating for 50 readers, has separate areas for consultation of original records, maps and microforms, with carrels for those using typewriters or computer equipment. Closed-circuit television supplements the normal staff invigilation. A separate meeting room is provided for school and other group visits.

A comfortable and pleasant working environment has been achieved both for public and staff, with carpeted floors throughout the building. Staff amenities include a generous staff room, a shower and a first aid room.

Cost: £2.3 million (excl. site).

Published references:
P Gill, 'West Sussex Record Office on the move', in *Society of Archivists Newsletter* 54 (Sept. 1990).

Unpublished: P Gill, *Report on the West Sussex Record Office* (1984).

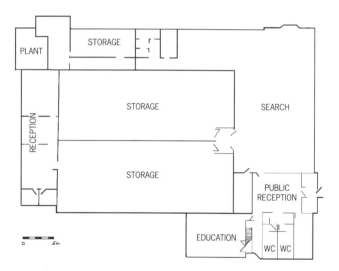

Appendix to Part 2

Archive buildings in the United Kingdom 1977–1992: checklist

The checklist below indicates the buildings and archive services in the public sector which have been taken into account in the preparation of this volume, for the most part constructed, converted or extended in the period. The list is arranged chronologically by year of occupation/official opening, or in a few cases appointment of the first archivist, depending on the source of information. An asterisk indicates that the premises are wholly or substantially purpose-built. Bold type indicates their inclusion as one of the case studies in part 2 of this volume. Published references to buildings not featured in the case studies are indicated in the footnotes to this appendix.

1977: Portsmouth City; **★PRO Kew**; Tyne and Wear.

1978: British Library of Political and Economic Science;[1] ★Bromley (in library); Dyfed – Carmarthen (in county hall).

1979: **★Cumbria – Barrow**; Gloucestershire;[2] Hull City; York City.

1980: **★Berkshire** (in shire hall); Clwyd – Ruthin (search room).

1981: Hampshire (phase 2 of church conversion);[3] Shakespeare Birthplace Trust.

1982: Devon – West Devon; **Doncaster** (phase 1); Durham Univ Dept of Palaeography (5 The College); Glamorgan – ★West Glamorgan (in county hall); **★Gwynedd – Caernarfon**; Humberside – South Humberside; Kent – Ramsgate (in library); ★Staffordshire (extension); Tate Gallery.[4]

1983: Aberdeen City (searchroom); **★Cornwall (extension)**; **East Sussex** (phase 1); ★Gloucestershire (extension);

Greater London; **Greater Manchester**; Shropshire Local Studies Library;[5] ★West Yorkshire – Calderdale (in library).[6]

1984: Cleveland; Derby Central Library; Wiltshire (extension); Strathclyde Region (in library).

1985: ★Barking & Dagenham (library extension); ★Birmingham Central Library (extension); **Cheshire** (phase 1); **Doncaster** (phase 2); ★Essex – Chelmsford (search room, strongroom annexe);[7] ★Essex – Colchester;[8] Grampian Region; **★Hereford & Worcester – Worcester HQ**; Kent – Maidstone (search room); ★Orkney (extension); Suffolk – Lowestoft (in library); West Yorkshire – Bradford.

1986: Barnsley (in library); British Geological Survey;[9] Clare College Cambridge; Coventry City;[10] ★Kent – Sevenoaks (in library);[11] **★National Library of Wales** (reading room); ★Redbridge (in library);[12] Walsall.[13]

1987: **Dumfries Archive Centre**; ★Gwynedd – Dolgellau (extension); **★National Film Archive J Paul Getty Jr Conservation Centre**; Richmond [London] (in library); **★Southampton University Library**.

1988: Borders Region (in library); ★Cardiff library (strongroom); Church of England Records Centre; **★Cornwall** (extension); Derbyshire; Dudley (phase 1); Girobank plc; **★Lancashire** (extension); National Museums and Galleries on Merseyside; **★North Devon** (in library); Oswestry; Sandwell (in library).

1989: Central Region; **Cheshire** (phase 2); **Glasgow University Business Records Centre**; Glamorgan – ★South Glamorgan (records centre in county hall); ★Lambeth Palace Library (extension); London Hospital; Merseyside; **Museum of Science and Industry, Manchester**; National Museum of Labour History, Manchester; National

Portrait Gallery; Oxfordshire (rebuilding on site); ★Royal Institution of Cornwall (strongroom); ★St Albans city; ★**Sheffield**; ★**West Sussex**; Wiltshire (extension).

1990: ★**BBC Written Archives**; British Telecom; Cambridgeshire – Huntingdon (refurbishment); ★Kent – Medway;[14] Northumberland – Berwick; Poole Borough (in civic centre); Powys;[15] Royal Greenwich Observatory (glass-plate negative archives); ★Royal Society (strongroom); Staffordshire – ★Lichfield; ★**Suffolk – Ipswich**; ★Sutton [London] (in library);[16] Weymouth district.

1991: British Library Oriental Collections (redevelopment); Bury [Gtr Manchester]; Dudley (phase 2); ★**Dorset**; ★**Lincolnshire**; ★**Northamptonshire**; Northumberland – Morpeth; **North Yorkshire**.

1992: Bristol; ★**Hammersmith & Fulham**; Hereford & Worcester – Hereford (redevelopment); **Post Office**.

Expected to open 1993: Brent (in library); ★**Hampshire**; Greater London (extension); ★Leicestershire; ★**Nottinghamshire**; ★Warwick University (Modern Records Centre).

Published references:
[Works cited by author only are included in the bibliography]

1. *LSE: The new library* (LSE pamphlet, 1978).

2. Gloucestershire *RO Report 1978–1979; Family Tree*, 1 no 2 (1985), p.22.

3. G Darley, 'Mass stacks', in *Architects' Journal*, 175 no 17 (1982), pp.32–5. M Risoluti, 'Chiesa vittoriano transformata in archivio di stato', in *L'industria delle costruzioni*, 135 (Jan 1983). Hampshire Record Office *Ten year report, 1974–1984* (1984).

4. S Fox-Pitt, 'The Tate Gallery Archive of twentieth-century British art, its formation and development', in *Archives*, 17 no 74 (Oct 1985), pp.97–8.

5. Harrison 1987, pp.182–4.

6. Harrison 1987, pp.32–4. M Dewe (ed) *A manual of local studies librarianship* (1987): illustrations pp.82, 86; plan p.160.

7. Essex Record Office *Update* 8 (Winter 1985/86). *Family Tree*, 2 no 3 (1986), pp.18–19.

8. Essex Record Office *Update* 7 (Summer 1985).

9. Harrison 1990, pp.60–2.

10. D Rimmer, 'Coventry City Record Office', in *Archives*, 19 no 84 (Oct 1990), pp.203–4.

11. Harrison 1990, pp.199–201. *Kent Archives Bulletin* 6 (1988).

12. 'Ilford Central Library', in Harrison 1990, pp.262–4.

13. See three articles each entitled 'Walsall Local History Centre', in *The Blackcountryman*, 20 no 3, pp.47–48; Library Association *Record*, 1987 p.589; and (by R Brown) in *Teaching History* (Oct 1987), p.5. Also L Tracey, 'Metro archives: what value?', in *Local History*, 17 (1988), pp.4–5.

14. Society of Archivists Newsletter, 56 (March 1991).

15. Society of Archivists Newsletter, 56 (March 1991).

16. 'Central Library, Sutton', Architects' Journal Building Study, 5 November 1980.

Synopsis of subjects in Part 1

Part 1 is arranged thematically. This is not a comprehensive index, but a means of bringing together useful secondary references. Rooms and functions are discussed in turn in chapter 9, and not all indexed here. Storage areas are mentioned in every chapter and not indexed.

Archive buildings
    character, 10–12, 17, 31, 45
    design/aesthetic considerations, 11,
        14–15, 17, 53–5, 58, 72
    shape, 31–2
    conversion or purpose building, ch 8;
        5, 6, 8, 33, 40, 44, 69
    conversion from
        school, 33, 36, 57–8, 71
        church, 58–9
        warehouse, 26, 55–7
    out-stores, 5, 6

Archives
    nature and importance, 1, 5, 10, 35,
        39, 47, 53, 55
    rate of accumulation, 5
    particular media:
        new media [film, sound etc], 3, 13,
        26, 37, 45–6, 51n, 64, 71
        cellulose nitrate, 19, 39

Environment, indoor, ch 7; 73
    air circulation/rate of change, 22,
        49–50, 54
    air-conditioning, 20, ch 7
    air quality/pollution, 13, 28, 48, 51n
    filtration and washing, 45–6, 48
    ventilation, 22, 23, 28, 46, 49
    control of temperature and relative
        humidity, ch 7; 11, 20–22, 58, 64
    lighting, 23, 52, 70, 74
    see also Structure: high thermal inertia

Environment, outdoor
    weather, 20, 47–8
    protection against, 20, 30

Environmental concern
    energy consumption, 2, 23, 24n, 28,
        50, 68
    gases in fire extinction, 41
    impact of buildings, 14–16, 32
    use of resources, 23, 53

Equipment
    computers, 6, 29, 34, 68

electrostatic dust-precipitators, 49
humidifiers/dehumidifiers, 22, 23,
    49–51
microfilm readers, 6, 29, 34, 70
shelving, 31, 64–6
    mobile, 20, 22, 26, 42, 49, 52, 58,
        65–6
    wooden, 64–5
telephones, 66, 69
see also ch 9 *passim*

Fire, *see* Hazards

Functions in an archive building
    checklist, ch 9; 62, 74
    relationships between, 11, ch 9; 72
    segregation of, 11, ch 9
    particular functions, ch 9;
        conservation, 11, 26, 30–1, 51, 66
        exhibition, 69–70
        plant, 11, 39, 66, 68–9
        public areas, 11, 31, 37–8, 42, 51,
        69–71
        reprographics, 11, 26, 31, 67
        staff offices, 11, 68

Hazards
    general, 1, 10, 11, 16
    associated with site, ch 2
    in particular:
        acidity, 46
        birds, 26, 28
        condensation, 21, 23, 26, 28
        dust, 13, 25, 26, 28, 32n, 40, 50, 54
        explosion, 13, 14
        fire, 13–14, ch 6; 65
            alarms, 18, 40
            compartments, 19
            detection, 40
            escapes, 19, 30, 44
            extinction, 18, 40–3
                gas, 18–19, 39, 40–3, 44n
                water, 19, 40–3, 44n, 63
                other, 42, 43
            resistance, 17–18, 30
        insects, 28, 30

light, 25, 28, 29, 30, 50, 52, 54, 57, 67, 70
lightning, 20, 37, 42
mould, 46–9, 63
    fumigation, 2, 63, 71n
noise, 13, 16, 61
pollutants, 13, 28, 46, 48, 51n, 63
terrorism, 19
theft, ch 5
vandalism, 30, ch 5; 54, 59n
water/flood, 13–14, 22, 26, 54
    alarms, 23, 24n, 68–9
    drainage, 22–3, 43
    waterproofing, 23, 27–8

Health and safety
    in general, 2, 11, 40–2, 54, 66–7, 73
    access by the disabled, 2, 55, 69, 73
    in particular:
        humidifier fever, 3, 50, 51n
        legionnaire's disease, 2, 50
        sick building syndrome, 3, 50

Materials, ch 3, ch 4

Planning
    in general, 5, 6
    role of architect, 10, 13, 72–4
    brief, 10, 12n, 72–4
    costs, 9–10, 58
    period of occupancy, 6
    problems, 6–7
    time scale, 5, 7–9

Security
    in general, ch 5; 2, 11, 19, 28, 30, 43, 73
    in shared buildings, 19, 54, 60
    in public areas, 35, 37–8, 70

    in WCs, 38
    degree of, 34–5
    coats and bags, 35, 37–8
    intruder alarms, 35, 36–7, 62
    locks, 37

Site
    in general, ch 2
    archaeology, 8, 15
    landscaping, 15

Structure
    in general, ch 3, ch 4, 73
    compartments, 19, 24n, 25, 47, 54–5, 57
    floor-loading, 19–20, 54–6
    foundations, 20, 54, 58
    high thermal inertia, 20–2, 45–6, 51n
    maintenance, 22
    particular features:
        air vents, 18, 26, 48
        ceilings, 25–6, 61, 70
        chimneys, 19, 54
        columns, 27, 38, 54
        doors, 19, 30–1, 37, 57
        drainpipes, 19
        fences, 36
        floors, 25–6, 49
            coverings, 26, 61, 67, 70
        lifts, 18, 31, 38, 55, 61, 69
        roofs, 20–1, 23, 28–9, 33, 47, 49, 54, 57–9
        stairs, 37–8, 55, 69
        walls, 25, 49, 54, 58, 61
            partitions, 25, 37, 71
        windows, 18–20, 22, 29–30, 48–50, 54

Printed in the United Kingdom for HMSO
Dd 293679 8/93